DEDICATED

to

NELLIE

My Wife, my Little Flower

my Friend, my Lover

my Sister in Christ

The Mother of my three daughters

And grandest of Grandmothers

Whose character

is as lovely

as her appearance

Whose life

has graced mine

and

the lives of all she has touched

Putting Music to the Words

Biblical Perspectives on Love, Courtship and Marriage

P 80 The best thing of all was that he was her friend with whom she could share everything.
P 81 - 85 The Shulamite is reflecting & learning a lot. She goes to him
P. 86 - He is kind & praises her.

P 99 - Ten ways he praises her
P 101 First she wanted to possess him now she stresses his possession of her & his desire toward her

A Commentary
On the Song of Solomon

P 109 love is priceless & indestructible

by Keith E. Knauss

P116 1:6 Her brothers apparently raised her from before she was a teenager 8:8. She was raised with character
Her brothers rented the vineyard from Solomon & put her to work in it. So Sol. met her.
P120 (8:14 The last word from her still eagerly waiting for his return to her which he did.
P121 – Love & marriage gone sour
P123, 124 Jesus forgave & gave new life
& hope John 4
& does today
P126 Hope –

Order From
MANNA MINISTRIES
1 North Herman Ave.
Auburn, NY 13021

© 1991 by Manna Ministries

Published by Manna Ministries

CONTENTS

FOREWORD

It is my desire that all who read this book could know the author, Dr. Keith E. Knauss. Not only is he my friend, but my best loved author. His God-given gift to write out of natural ability, and use the English language so smoothly and in such flowing, loving manner, is thrilling.

Because I am a Christian Psychologist and Family Counselor, I am often called upon for advice and counsel in family matters. Yet, as I read this book, "Putting Music To The Words", I became vividly aware that; not only has God truly given us a commentary on the subject of Courtship and Marriage in the Song of Solomon, but He has also given, in Dr. Knauss, one of the best minds to understand and expound those great Scriptures.

To meet Dr. Knauss, his lovely wife and sweet family, is to see and understand that he is a natural for God to show great wisdom through and to teach the great revelations found in the Song of Solomon.

I wholeheartedly recommend this book as a vivid exposure and teaching on great love relationships.

Dr. William L. Johnson, Ph.D.
Christian Psychologist,
Pastor, Teacher, Counselor

PREFACE

Without controversy the Bible is the Book of Books. Moreover our hearts confirm that the Song of Solomon is the Book of the Book! Although there is not one Book of the Old Testament that makes reference to the Song of Solomon, nor one Book of the New Testament that so much as gives a quotation from it, and though, like the Book of Esther, there is not found a single reference to God in it, yet it has ever been deemed holy to the Jews who placed it among their sacred writings. Years later our Lord placed the Divine seal upon this Book when He said, "Search the Scriptures...for they are they which testify of me." He thus verified and settled once for all, the place of the Song of Solomon in the Hebrew Canon of Scripture.

The Song of Solomon is a song of true love and, by keeping Solomon in mind as a type of Christ seeking His Bride, we may expect to see in this little Book a rich unveiling of the heart of Him who is our heavenly lover.

Fittingly this song follows the Book of Ecclesiastes where the story of failure and disappointment in the flesh causes the writer to exclaim, "All is vanity and vexation of spirit." Solomon's song causes the heart to soar above and beyond itself until all its desire and satisfaction is found in the Beloved. Likewise the seventh chapter of Romans sets forth nothing but failure and disappointment in the flesh, while the eighth chapter reveals all joy and love in Christ. So here the divine Bridegroom becomes the object of the heart, in contrast to the failure of the flesh.

A writer of times past wrote, "If you would be holy, read the Psalms. If you would be wise, read the Proverbs. But if you would learn love's language, and understand all action of love to establish real lasting communion, read the Song of Songs and breathe the fragrant air that surrounds the utterances of the King of Love to His Bride."

As for us who still are part of the pilgrimage in these final days of the Age of Grace, we agree to all of the above and clasp

3

the Song of Solomon to our hearts as the Book which sets forth the beauty and preciousness of our lovely Lord as does no other. Moreover, we hold that this Book, which has remained so misunderstood and neglected, is surely the Book designed for us as we travel through a world gone mad with lust and substitute love. The God who created us and instituted the Home, did not leave us in the dark concerning Love, Courtship, Marriage and Sex. He provided us with specific plans for our pleasure and profit. His plans!

To study the Song of Solomon is to discover that God intended Love and Marriage to bring a touch of heaven to the heart and home. God not only gave man a song to sing, but provided the musical accompaniment.

Keith E. Knauss

Chapter One

THE SETTING FOR THE SONG

We approach the Song of Solomon with a pervading sense of reverence and reserve. Feelings of both awe and anticipation cause us to hesitate upon the threshold. The still small voice speaks to our hearts; and we feel the need to remove our shoes, for we are about to walk on holy ground. Matters of life sacred to God are to be dealt with here. God's song of love will be seen exemplified in human setting The Song of Solomon, without controversy, is a very neglected Book. Many who teach it are found guilty of the grave mistake of making Israel seen as the Bride. Israel is the wayward wife of Jehovah, but never the Bride. The Bride is always the Church of Jesus Christ!

Revered commentators have been known to advise young and inexperienced ministers to avoid preaching on the Song of Solomon. That is strange counsel! Such advise is out of harmony with God's intention.

In II Tim. 3:16 Paul declares, "All Scripture is given by inspiration of God, and is profitable for doctrine" (teaching)! The word "all" in that verse certainly includes the Song of Solomon. Be assured that one may read this little Book and know God's mind. Solomon's Song will reprove us, correct us, and instruct us in righteousness. It will prove entirely profitable.

Paul also wrote, "For whatsoever things were written aforetime were written for our learning" (Rom. 15:4). The Song of Solomon is surely included in that "whatsoever"! And it does offer so much that we need to learn.

There is perhaps no more mysterious Book in the Bible than the Song of Solomon. However that is no valid excuse to avoid it. The mystery ministers in that it calls for an attitude of complete dependence upon the Holy Spirit, the divinely appointed Teacher. He is the Revealer of all Truth (I Cor. 2:9- 10). May He be pleased to reveal His mind and desires as to Love and Marriage, as well as lift the veil on the things of Christ, in this wonderful song. May our lives be forever changed for good.

1:1 - "The Song"

The initial words provide the character of the book. The Book is a song! Furthermore it is a LOVE SONG! A song of pure, holy, wholesome, refreshing, and uplifting love.

Love is ordained of God.

LOVE IS THE HIGHEST, HOLIEST, NOBLEST PASSION THAT A HUMAN IS CAPABLE OF EXPERIENCING! This writing deals with a love concerning which there is nothing sordid, degrading, or shameful. The love spoken of here is far superior to the type of love we hear about and see portrayed before us today.

The love of this Song is altogether in keeping with the divine Author who inspired Solomon to write it.

"The Song of Songs"!

This phrase suggests the superiority of the Book. It is of superior excellence! The Spirit of God employs this idea often in Scripture. For example, God is called "THE GOD OF GOD'S" in order to convey to us that He is the supreme God. The Lord is referred to as "THE LORD OF LORD'S" to indicate He is the supreme Lord. Christ is called "THE KING OF KING'S to testify He is the supreme King. We read of "THE HEAVEN OF HEAVENS" denoting the supreme heaven. Thus, "THE SONG OF SONGS" carries the idea that this writing is the supreme song from the pen of man. "The Song of Songs" suggests God's estimate and value of the Book.

What God places first, let no man supplant.

It is the Song of Songs because it is divinely inspired. God inspired other writings and songs, but hereby declares that this is Prince of them all.

It is the Song of Songs because it so glorifies our lovely Lord

Jesus. It is the story of Christ's love for you and me. Make its music yours.

"The Song of Songs which is Solomon's"!

Solomon is the human writer; the Holy Spirit the divine Author. It is assumed this Book was written early in Solomon's career; obviously at a time when his heart was yet tender to the Lord. Later it was not so (I Kings 11:4). Despite Solomon's foolish defection in later times, God said he was the wisest man who ever lived.

Follow the footsteps of the flock through this Book and you will increasingly become aware of the heavenly wisdom that prevails as Solomon personifies Him who is the wisdom of God. This is not a song of fools; though many love songs must be so classified. At the outset of the Song we are introduced, one by one, to the characters involved in the story. Note them:

1:2 - First is a peasant girl which we shall refer to as the SHULAMITE. Her voice is the first to be heard.

1:4 - The second personage is the KING. This is none other than Solomon himself (see also 1:12).

1:7 - The third performer is a SHEPHERD to whom the Shulamite speaks in this verse. Let it be known that the King plays two roles in this story. He wears two outfits. He Appears as both Shepherd and King! In both roles he courts the Shulamite without her being aware that the Shepherd and the King are the same person.

1:6 - The fourth part is played by Sulamite's FAMILY. She briefly alludes to them.

1:5 - The fifth category is assigned the WOMEN OF SOLOMON'S COURT; spoken of as the "daughters of Jerusalem".

7

3:3 - The sixth and last of the performers are the WATCH-MEN OF THE CITY; picturing this present world. The watch-men do so much to discourage and hinder true love.

Consider a prefacing critique on the development of love in this story. While the peasant girl is tending the family vine-yards, she meets and falls in love with a shepherd. Her family strongly opposes the courtship (1:6-7). "My mother's children were ANGRY with me!" Surely they did not dream that one so beautiful and so talented would marry a man so poor. What a nerd he must be! But when the wise King took a fancy to her, and invited her to his court, they probably reacted with, "My, how good God is!"

Though the Shulamite is in the King's house, the Shepherd is in her heart! She resists every attention of the King because of love for her Shepherd (cf 1:4 and 1:12-13). She assures her shep-herd lover that her mind is wholly occupied with him, and that they will live in remembrance of their love and rejoice and be glad in it (1:4). Even while sitting at the King's table the fra-grance of her love for the Shepherd is ascending (1:12). It was something like sitting with your date while holding hands with another.

Of course that wonderful day finally arrived when the King was manifested as none other than the Shepherd lover, and the Shulamite joyfully claimed him and gave herself completely to him.

The lesson sets forth the transcendent truth that Jesus Christ is both King (Jh. 18:37) and Shepherd (Jh. 10:11), and that BE-FORE WE CAN RIGHTFULLY CLAIM HIM AS KING, WE MUST COME TO CONFESS AND LOVE HIM AS SHEPHERD; the Shepherd "Who giveth His life for His sheep."

Many hold Jesus Christ as Saviour who fail to hail Him as King! Those who do receive Christ as their Shepherd must come to recognize and own Him as their King.

The Shulamite pictures the believer so well. While she rec-ognized her lover in shepherd garments, she was unable to discern him in kingly robes. Could it be so with us that though Christ is our Saviour, we may not yet know Him as Lord? The fruit of love in our lives is when the Shepherd received becomes the King realized: And that is when the music begins.

Chapter Two

PLAY THE PRELUDE PLEASE

Now is the time to start putting music to the words. In order to do this we need to consider the mind of God on the subject of love, courtship and marriage.. Would you believe it possible for man to understand much of the nature of God through love! That is why God allowed us to know and experience love.

Whenever the nature of God is mentioned, or the Trinity is introduced, thick fog seems to settle on the minds of most people. They cannot quite grasp the truth as to how three can be one! To explain the Trinity theologians give such examples as steam, water and ice, all being water. Or they point out the three sides of a triangle as still being one triangle. These illustrations all fall short, for the Scripture is not teaching that God is one person existing in three forms, but that each Person of the Godhead is FULLY GOD!

Quite interesting also is the fact that God never illustrated the Trinity, though He came close a couple of times. Would you believe that the illustration God gives of Himself is THE MARRIAGE RELATIONSHIP! For example, in Genesis 1:26 God said, "let US make man in OUR image." The word "us" assumes that there is more than one person in the ONE God! Then in Genesis 1:27, "God created man in His own image, in the image of God created He him, MALE AND FEMALE created He them." You will readily note that Man plus Woman equals MAN! One plus one equals ONE; for the two shall become one flesh! Again in Genesis 2:24 it describes the married couple as "ONE flesh." Two, yet one!

The New Testament picks up on that and enlarges the truth. "The head of every man is Christ; and the head of the woman is the man; and the head of Christ is God" (I Cor. 11:3). IN SOME

11

WAY THE FATHER RELATES TO THE SON AS THE HUS-BAND RELATES TO HIS WIFE! Perhaps the way is that in both cases while there is Equality there is also Leadership! The Father is equal to the Son but the Father initiates and the Son delights to do His will. Likewise the husband initiates and the wife delights to respond to his will. The Trinity is the reality of which Marriage is the shadow!

Where then does the Spirit come in? Well, where there is love there is a trinity; a Lover, a Beloved and the Spirit of Love. The spirit of love between a couple may well provide the illustration of the Spirit of God.

Thus God seems to lift the curtain to allow us a faint glimpse of the relationship of love that existed before the world began. Christ said, "Thou lovest me before the foundation of the world" (John 17:24). Here some will ask the question, "How could there be such a thing as a loving God before there were people to love?"

Some suggest God created man so that He might have someone to love. Nonsense! To say that is to fail to recognize that GOD IS LOVE! He does not need us that He might love. His love is independent of us. He does not need us to love, but we desperately need Him to love us!

The truth is, it is you and I who need someone to love us and, in turn, we need someone to love. God knew that so He gave Eve to Adam and instituted Marriage and Home. And how wonderful it is when the all-wise God brings into our lives the right one for us to love, and who loves us in return. That is what makes life and home worthwhile.

It is in LOVE that peace and joy are found (Gal. 5:22). And there is no feeling like the security and peace found in mutual love.

Though we know it works both ways, psychologists tell us that the best thing a husband can do for his children is to LOVE THEIR MOTHER! Those children will then know that the foundation of their home is based on a love independent of them! They will sense that no matter what happens, their home will withstand every storm.

In the same fashion, upon recognizing that God HIMSELF IS LOVE and that His love is eternal, we can rest in the blessed fact that nothing which has happened or shall happen, will ever be able to separate us from His love in Christ Jesus (Rom. 8:38-39). Therein is our peace and security.

As a boy at home I knew my father and mother loved each other. We watched their romantic antics and grinned like Cheshire cats thinking we had been let in on something extra special. I knew I was loved because I was their child! So God is my Father and He loves me because He loves His Son my Saviour. My salvation is founded on a love between them. It is a love that goes on independent of me. I am just the blessed recipient of their love.

THE SHULAMITE GIRL FOUND WHAT IT WAS TO REST IN AN UNCHANGING LOVE. She went through times of doubt, fear, indifference, hurts, etc. , but finally came to full rest in the knowledge that her Beloved loved her with a true unchanging love. He did not wring his hands when she faltered or failed. Nor does God come apart at the seams when we fail or step out of line. Instead, in overflowing love, He graciously and patiently brings us to a new experience of His love.

If you like True Romances, you will revel in this one.

Play the Prelude please!

13

Chapter Three

THE MAKING OF MEMORIES

Love is something that is born within us and it takes time to develop. Too often people act in haste and repent at leisure. Quick on romance may mean long on regret. But if there ever was anything in life that needed TIME and PATIENCE it is the matter of falling in love and preparing for marriage.

Years ago a young couple came on New Year's Eve and asked to be married then and there. Time was of the essence as he was due to report back to the naval base in another day. When I inquired how long they had known each other they said, "We just met tonight and know we are meant for each other!" Of course they had no license and could not be lawfully married. Believe it or not, they never did get married. But they thought that night that they had fallen in love!

Today people seem to be falling OUT of love as easily and often as falling IN love. Too often we hear the words, "I have fallen out of love with my wife (or husband)." And generally such resent the advice, "Well then, fall in love with them again!"

You can learn to love (Titus 2:4)! And you can learn to love your wife or husband all over again! The truth is when someone says they have fallen out of love with their spouse it is generally because they have "fallen in love" with someone else.

The frightening truth is that many married couples have never really known what it is to "fall in love" with each other. They just got married, and their marriage is based on Duty and Responsibility which, of course, is essential, BUT all many couples have going for them is the fact of a past ceremony, a back seat full of kids and a few years of togetherness under their belt. They are living together in a relationship that is far less than what God intended. They know nothing of ROMANCE which is imperative in every marriage. The Song of Solomon makes that abundantly clear.

True, marriage is based on commitment and, if no romance exists, it still is a marriage. But as we read the Song of Solomon we understand that God's intention of marriage is more than vows spoken before two or three witnesses. It is to be characterized by romance....a commitment to continual courtship!

Do not become apathetic to the necessity of mutual romance. Romance puts the music in marriage! It makes love beautiful!! It causes the heart to sing!

1:1 - "The Song of Songs"

What a way to open a story of True Romance! Romance, God's way, is filled with the sound of music; the music of love. Love that abides will always hear melody.

After my wife's mother passed away, my father-in-law said, "The song is over but the melody lingers." What a tribute to their abiding love. And that is the way it should be. Love is a ministry of music.

Without real romance, without real love between the married couple, there is lack of needed communication; for we truly communicate with each other by loving.

Here is a song with 117 verses! Most worshipers hate to stand in church and sing all four verses of a hymn. But let's sing all the stanzas of Solomon's Song.

The Song of Solomon is par excellence on Romance. It holds needed guidelines for singles as well as married. Regrettably this book is ignored to a great degree and those who seek love try to experience what is found in movies, magazines or novels and, generally, that is love without reality and morals. Solomon gives us God's viewpoint on love, marriage and sex, and tells us how "falling in love" should happen when God's love is controlling us and when His principles determine our feelings.

By the way, the Song of Solomon portrays MAN as the lover He is the romanticist; tender in his approach, lavish in his praise, sensitive to his spouse's needs. Every wife needs the romancing of her husband and this book expresses that. Macho men can learn how to be romantic, how to love. Believe it! You can stay in love or you can fall in love all over again, even if the bloom of the honeymoon has long since faded.

When was Romance born for you? Does the memory warm your heart? I recall how it happened for me. I had courted a lovely christian girl from Bible College but, as sure as the sun shines, God spoke to say she was not the one for me. How I dreaded to break off our relationship. Later I met the Little Flower, Nellie. She was a Heavenly Vision and I was not disobedient to it. When I saw her I KNEW she was the one (just like Mother said I would). The butterflies were stirred that day.

Those days of courtship were wonderful and we took loads of pictures. We still love to look at them. There are pictures of us together; some I took of her alone and some she took of me. I snapped some of her in feigned poses and smiles and some in faded jeans and some in fancy clothes. We have picnic scenes and scenic shots. The pictures she took always seemed to catch me acting like a fool or trying to make a big impression. But the pictures of our wedding day, when she came down the aisle on the arm of her Dad, dressed so beautifully in that gown of exquisite white, looking the absolute personification of loveliness, then standing beside me beneath that lilac covered archway; those pictures are priceless.

You might be able to put together the story of our courtship by placing the pictures in order. In the same way we can place the photographs of the courtship of Solomon and the Shulamite together and capture their romance. But then Solomon has already done this for us. Solomon has arranged nine choice photos that tell the story of romance with the one who became his Queen.

Remember, however, that this account was written AFTER the marriage. How long after we do not know, but what is important is that Solomon is still gleaning comfort and pleasure from their courtship. Muse with me over their photo album.

I.   Picture #1 reveals THE CHARACTER OF THE BE-LOVED (1:1-4).

It would mean this picture was taken by the Bride.

1:2 - "Kiss me."

There is nothing like the joy of first love! He who has once tasted that first love in Christ can but long for more. Kiss me! We see here that Solomon occupies the role of LEADERSHIP; a role the Shulamite not only accepts but encourages!

Note that the Song has no introduction. It just commences with the revelation of the Bride's intense longing for the One her heart loved and longed for. She desired his love more than anything!

Kiss me! Imagine God wanting to kiss me! Do you marvel that He even loves you? In ancient times it was an honor if a king permitted his hand or garment to be kissed by his subjects. If he kissed another, mouth to mouth, this was taken to be the GREATEST of all honors he could bestow! His kiss was to her the highest honor!

"Kiss me...Draw me" (vv2,4). She feels the force of his love.

1:4 - "The King hath brought me into his chambers..."

In this story it seems she is abruptly snatched from her shepherd lover and taken to the King's court. Solomon would test her love and faithfulness. It is not until Solomon is satisfied that the Shulamite loves him for what he IS, and not merely for what he can GIVE, that he reveals his true identity. He has already won her Hand. Now he wants to win her Heart.

However, the luxuries of the palace do not change her feelings for the Shepherd. She wants only his love. "Let him kiss me with the kisses OF HIS MOUTH!" She wants no higher honor than his love. That alone satisfies her.

1:2 - "For thy love is better than wine."

She had made her choice. Wine is considered earth's best, but to the Shulamite, Solomon's love was better than the best! In like manner, Christ's love is superior to the best offered by this world. Moses was a man who knew this, for he esteemed "the reproach of Christ greater riches than the treasures of Egypt" (Heb. 11:26).

1:3 - "Because of the savour of thy good ointments..."

She not only loved his kisses, but his cologne! He always smelled good. Men, be wise and remember that.

"Thy name is an ointment."

His life was sweet and fragrant, like his name implied. And what a name! No wonder we sing, "Take the world but give me JESUS!" What a lovely name. In this Book, Solomon has no other name but "Beloved" and "My love".

"Thy name is an ointment POURED FORTH."

He gives HIMSELF! Did you know the first mention of fragrance in the Bible is found in Gen. 8:21-22. It is in connection with the Burnt Offerings Noah placed on the altar and which rose to the Lord as a "sweet savor". It is ever a picture of God giving HIMSELF (as at Isaac's offering).

And is not the giving of oneself the picture of love? You go on living for yourself and then, suddenly there is one in your life to whom you want to GIVE YOURSELF! Then you live a life of giving because of loving. In the pouring out of yourself comes the fragrance of love.

"Poured forth."

Solomon was not only handsome, one that "ALL the virgins love" but it was the INNER MAN poured out which made him so attractive. He had character!

THE ONE YOU MARRY SHOULD BE THE KIND OF PERSON YOU CAN RESPECT!

II. Picture #2 reveals THE CHARACTER OF THE BRIDE (1:5-7).

Notice that when she realized how wonderful Solomon was, she became aware of her NOTHINGNESS!

1:5 - "I am black..."

She was beautiful or Solomon would not have given her a second look. But above her beauty, see her humility.

"I am black as the tents of Kedar."

Had she been too long under the sun in the vineyards (vs 6)? She had become as black as the tents of Kedar. Kedar is the second of Ishmael's twelve sons (Gen. 25:13). Ishmael is a type of flesh (Gal. 4:23). The Shulamite then is reflecting upon her natural state, before the mighty work of grace was wrought in her heart.

She saw herself as BLACK, but he saw her as the "fairest among women" (vs 8). The nearer we find ourselves to Him whom we love, the more conscious we are of our sinful condition. Job said, now mine eye seeth thee...wherefore I abhor myself" (Job 42:5-6).

"I am black , BUT..."

Though black she saw herself as comely as the curtains of Solomon. In the same breath in which she confesses her worthlessness, she asserts her **loveliness!** What a blessed "BUT..."It reveals the work of grace in her life.

She says I am comely as Solomon's curtains. The "curtains" may refer to the brilliant colored curtains in the palace, or the VEIL of the Temple (seen only from WITHIN)! Beneath the blackness was an unsurpassable beauty! C. H. Spurgeon said, "Never make more of your sins than you do of your Saviour."

1:6 - "They made me keeper of the vineyards, but mine own vineyard have I not kept."

She felt she had not had time to keep her personal appearance looking good. Ladies, you OUGHT to take the time! It will be well worth the effort.

1:7 - "Tell me...for why should I be as one that turneth aside..."

This shows her good character and the respect she had for his good name as well as her own reputation. In that culture one that turned aside meant a "veiled woman"; or a prostitute. If she were going to meet her lover she wanted it to be "AT NOON"; at the proper place and time! She would allow no shadow to fall on his good name, or on their relationship.

"Tell me where..."

Let nothing be kept from me! The Shulamite did not want to

go wandering about looking for him, appearing to be aggressive and available to anyone. She did not want to do anything suggesting compromise or contradiction. SHE APPRECIATED RIGHT THINGS! Her character was sterling and beautiful.

III. Picture #3 reveals HER COMPANIONSHIP WITH THE KING (1:8-11).

In this photo we see how special the Shulamite was to Solomon. It also reveals the steps he took to overcome her sense of INSECURITY; to make her feel special and loved.

1:8 - "O thou fairest among women..."

Imagine her feelings. She is beside the King and must feel horrid about the way she looks, all the while knowing that those highbrowed women of the palace court are staring at her. She must say, "Oh look at me! I feel so stupid!"

Solomon now speaks. This is the first recorded utterance of the bridegroom, and it is the outpouring of his heart, "O thou fairest among women!" What grace it showed to the poor maiden who thought so little of herself. The keen perception of love enabled Soloman to see deeper than mere outward appearance. Love looks on the heart, and by its very appreciation of the beloved's inner graces beholds more beauty of character. It evokes praise.

By the way men, your wife needs not only to think she looks good to you, but to hear you say it. Solomon saw in her the most wonderful girl in the world and he did not keep his feelings silent. He expressed those feelings in praise to her.

1:9 - "To a mare among the Chariots of Pharaoh, I liken you my darling."

Solomon is not simply using flattery, he speaks the truth. We are not suggesting that any man liken his wife to a horse; for it could backfire. But the Shulamite understood the illustration. The greatest splendor of the time was to view the beautifully formed and lavishly bedecked chariot horses of Pharaoh's court. Imported from Egypt they were marvels of swiftness and symmetry; each one garnished with gold and precious stones worthy of a king's ransom. And of course Pharaoh had the cream of the crop.

Solomon had her grace and beauty and royalty in mind. The chariots of Pharaoh were pulled by several pairs of prize horses and the PRIZE MARE of all was in the lead position. She was in the lead because she was more beautiful and noble than the rest. Thus was the Shulamite in the eyes of Solomon. And so must the wife know that she is that special in the eyes of her husband.

1:10 - "Thy cheeks are comely with rows of jewels...chains of gold."

Solomon seems to sense her feeling of poor appearance and tells her that she does not need adornment. She is a natural beauty. She has been harnessed with the gold and silver of nature.

1:11 - "We will make thee borders of gold with studs of silver."

The ladies of the court also sense her feelings and, seeing how the king loves her, they tell her they will make the best adornment for her. They had ridiculed her (vs 8) when she asked of them where her Shepherd kept his flock; but now they understand she is the one who is all important to the king and so will adorn her with silver (redemption) and gold (glory).

A picture of the Bride is given in Rev. 21:11, which leaves us breathless and speechless at the sight of such grace, "Having the glory of God, and her light was like unto a stone, even like a jasper stone, clear as crystal."

But note how SENSITIVE Solomon is to her needs! He is "touched" by her feelings of infirmity, and so verbally assures her of the special place she has in his heart! She is FIRST of all to him! And he sees to it she is provided with everything that is necessary to make her feel wanted and loved by him, and at home with him. Like our Lord, he supplied all her need.

IV. **Picture #4 reveals THE CONTEMPLATION OF LOVE**

(1:12-14)

The Shulamite is remembering her shepherd lover. We might call it "day dreaming". She is sitting at the king's table, which is surrounded by dignitaries and officials discussing national affairs, and the women of the court are chatting over social events. As the buzzing drones on she loses herself in thought as she remembers her shepherd lover. She lives "in remembrance of him."

The king has not swept her off her feet by possibilities of fame and fortune. Despite her shepherd's apparent poverty, she prefers him to the king. Three things keep her steadfast and immovable in her love for the Shepherd amid all the enticements and alluring splendors of the palace.

a. Meditation (vv 12-14). Her shepherd is to her as precious myrrh.

b. Rumination (vv 15). She recalls how her shepherd lover sees her.

c. Anticipation (vv 16-17). Home is not where she lives, but where she loves! Where he is, there she wants to be. Anywhere so long as he is there. And as she thinks of her shepherd lover she cannot help but softly smile at what crosses her mind; for while she is being courted by the king, she is loving her shepherd!

1:12 - "My spikenard sendeth forth the fragrance thereof."

It is as though she says, "You would like this Chanel #5 I am wearing for you. The king seeks my love, but I want to be a sweet savour only to you."

1:13 - "A pouch of myrrh is my beloved unto me; he shall lie all night between my breasts."

Common in the culture of that day was the practice of women wearing a small pouch of perfume around their neck which constantly produced a fragrant aroma. The Shulamite was wearing one and it prompted this thought. She is saying that her thoughts of the shepherd lover were as sweet as the fragrance coming from the pouch between her breasts, and she would not remove it at night, but wear it so that her thoughts

23

would always be of him. This was like David, who in thinking of his Lord said, "On my bed will I meditate!"

1: 14 - **"My beloved is unto me as a cluster of camphire in the vineyards of En-gedi."**

A cluster of camphire was used as an ornament. The implication here is that her Beloved adorns her life...he sweeps her off her feet!

En-gedi was an oasis in a desert wilderness. One could walk through desert wastes for miles, where nothing grew, then suddenly come upon the welcome sight of En-gedi. The Shulamite is saying the world was like a wilderness without him. He was to her as a refreshing oasis.

But even more precious than an oasis in a desert, he was to her as the LOVELIEST of flowers in that oasis! He was like the delicate henna blossoms (known as the Flower of Paradise). So our Lord Jesus is to us in this world.

V. Picture #5 reveals THE CONVERSATION OF LOVE (1:15 - 2:3).

One needs a long range lens here, as the couple is taking one of their walks in the country.

1:15 - **"Behold...Behold...Behold.."**

The word "behold" is found three times here; twice in verse 15 and again in verse 16. Solomon uses that word to call her attention to her own beauty. "Behold" (WOW)!

"Thou art fair my love...thou art fair; thou hast dove's eyes"!

The eyes are said to be the transparencies through which the soul looks. Apparently they are looking into each other's eyes as they speak. And as Solomon looks into her eyes he is reminded of dove's eyes. The eyes of a dove DILATE at the sight of their mate! I know it is true. When I asked the Little Flower to marry me we were sitting on a clover covered hill. I popped her the question, and do you know what happened? A mosquito bit me! But when I looked into those eyes, those lovely brown eyes, she looked so deep into mine I thought she could see forever; and so help me, her eyes dilated!

1:16-2:1 - "Behold thou art fair my beloved, yea, pleasant..."

Look at her response! She hastens to assure him that it is HE that is fair, and more than that, pleasant! She is telling him how handsome he is. It is hard for two who are in love to hold back their feelings for each other. In fact it becomes almost painful not to express it. He is initiating, and she is responding.

"Our couch is green".

She calls it "our" couch and ever green. It was always restful and peaceful to be with him. It seems they loved to be alone on some wooded path. She likened the green grass, on which they sat, to be their couch. And she likened the branches of the cedar tree above them to be the rafters of their house, etc.

Why is it that so much courting is done out among the things of nature? And why is it that once folks get married they seem to forget to go again to those early places of courtship and walk down those same paths while holding hands? Of course, you may not feel up to walking so far now, and you may have to stop and rest more often, but DO IT!

2:1 - "I am the rose of Sharon, and the lily of the valleys."

What has love done to her? Remember she had said, "I AM BLACK...". Now the view of herself has changed. She says, "I am the rose of Sharon, and the lily of the valleys." We are what we are by the grace of God.

2:2 - "But as the Lily among THORNS..."

Solomon seems to put a finger to her lips to stop her words, and adds, "But as the lily among thorns." She is to him as DISTINCT as a lily among thorns (among the unregenerate, the cursed)! All other women were as thorns compared to her.

The lily is not at home among thorns, but even there she can bloom for him and shed her sweetness around. Our Lord also saw us as a treasure is a field, a lily in the valley, and as the pearl of great price in a sea.

How uplifted she must have felt to hear him describe how special she was to him.

2:3 - "As the apple tree among the trees....so is my beloved among the sons.."

She responds again to say there are none like unto him! He stands out among all.

"I SAT DOWN" - You are my REST.

"UNDER HIS SHADOW" - You are my REFUGE.

"HIS FRUIT IS SWEET" - You are my REFRESHING.

"WITH GREAT DELIGHT" - You are my REJOICING.

The Shulamite is testifying that she came out of the sun and he was like the shadow of an apple tree to her, and that she found in him the sweetest fruit. He is everything she needed and ever will need. EVERY GIRL WHO FALLS IN LOVE SHOULD FIND REST AND FULFILLMENT IN THE ONE SHE LOVES...AND IN NO OTHER! He alone is everything!

VI. Picture #6 reveals THE CROWING OF LOVE (2:4-7).

Gaze long at this picture for it reveals the Shulamite radiantly in love. And as we keep all the pictures in mind, we see their courtship unfolds a steady movement towards marriage.

2:4 - "He brought me to the banqueting house."

Love's experience deepens. No longer just his shadow, or fruit, but now His house. Most feel this is a type of the House of the Lord. Today some would refer to the House of the Lord as the church. By the way ladies, do not marry a man who is not in fellowship with God's people. It is so important.

"His banner over me is LOVE!"

Now she does not mean Solomon had some huge banner like those displayed at football games, on which was printed the word LOVE which he held high over her head. Not at all. The banner she speaks of refers to that high, wide banner used in BATTLE! When the troops needed to regroup, this banner was raised so all could see where to assemble. This kind of banner was used in great marches where hundreds of people were divided up and guided by the position of the banner over them. It was like a gigantic traveling billboard.

Understanding begins to penetrate our minds. The Shulamite is saying that the love which Solomon has for her is PUBLICLY EVIDENT to all. Solomon does not say one thing to her in private, then contradict it in public. He is not caring when they are alone and cold when they are with others. He is never ashamed of his love for her. He wants the world to know of his love for her. Little wonder she grew secure in his love.

Our Lord also has the right to display His love banner over us. What a story it tells. Love was a willing victim. Love suffered, loved died, and now love would bring us to His royal feast where we may sit at His table and revel in His love. Love has conquered all our foes; why not let it conquer us?

The Shulamite is head over heals in love with Solomon. So much so that she becomes lovesick! She has grown weak from her increasing devotion to this man.

2:5 - "Sustain me...refresh me...for I am· FAINT WITH LOVE"!

She loves Solomon so much she can hardly stand it! Realization dawns on her that she is at the point where resistance is low: that she is desiring to express her love in the fullest way. Therefore we hear her sighing--

2:6 -- "His left hand is under my head, and his right doth embrace me."

His LEFT hand to love and His RIGHT hand to hold! This is not a statement of fact, but an expression of desire. Now think a bit. Love has advanced to the point where she wants and needs all of him. Anyone who can share years in a courtship and not long to know their lover intimately, probably does not truly love them! Are there any with heart and soul so dead, and love so unresponsive, that they did not look forward to fullness in love with their lover in marriage? It is natural.

The Shulamite's words reveal that for his left hand to be under her head, and his right hand embracing her, they would have be to lying down. A couple must realize their love will develop to that extent...SO THERE MUST BE RESTRAINT! And as their marriage draws nearer, the more restraint becomes necessary. And true love will display restraint. Hence--

2:7 - "I Charge you...by the roes and by the hinds of the field that ye STIR NOT UP, nor awaken love..."

To stir up sleeping roes or hinds would be to have them gone; racing away out of control. Leave them be for the time. Do not force this development of love. To force a flower to blossom ahead of time would only tear and ruin the petals. Let the flower develop as God intended, and it will be beautiful.

After all, no decision to marry should be based on sexual passion. A mattress is a poor foundation for marriage. Solomon loved the Shulamite for what SHE WAS, not for what she might be like in bed. Oh, the lovely character of these two.

However, we all understand that sex is an integral part of marriage. And she is at the stage where she wants to marry this man and give herself to him. Yet she realized that she must CONTROL those desires and not force the relationship prematurely. Sex would come naturally in its own time. Thus after experiencing the most intense longing of her courtship, the Shulamite gives some sound advice about PATIENCE. "Love suffereth long...doth not behave itself unseemly...beareth all things...endureth all things..." You can wait! Love has the grace to be patient.

Never succumb to wrong desire. Take the time of courtship to know one another in other ways. Like walking in the woods together...enjoying each other's company...laughing and learning together. It is important to find out--

* If they really love the Lord.

* If they are lazy.

* If they are unclean about their person.

* If they are untidy, or bossy, or mannerly.

* How they value children. Do they want a family? This is a matter that needs to be settled prior to marriage. Did you know that the average woman spends 32% of her life as a mother? That means twenty-five years out of a possible seventy! There must be agreement on this matter.

* If you respect each other! The word "reverence" in Ephesians 5:33 is translated RESPECT! God says respect must be seen to. It would appear that if a couple does not genuinely respect each other, they cannot truly love each other!

The wise advice of the Shulamite is to all. Do not stir up sexual desire prematurely, then base a decision to marry on the strength of that desire. Keep thyself with all diligence. Wear the crown of love royally, with head held high.

VII. **Picture #7 reveals THE CRAZINESS OF LOVE (2:8-14).**

Love makes calendars and clocks deceiving. When you are young time appears not to progress. The Shulamite probably thought the time for marriage would never arrive; that it seemed as far away as forever. We all were that anxious. In Bible College the students all prayed for the Lord to hasten His coming; but not until after they were married!

When in love time does seem to stand still. A few days between phone calls is like month! Weekend to weekend is more like six years instead of six days. I know whereof I speak! I suspect the Shulamite wondered when she and her shepherd lover would be together again. Then one glorious spring day he arrived, and it was their most delightful time thus far. Her patience was rewarded.

This photo, believe it or not, appears to be in Kodak color. The lilt of Spring is in the air. Everything in nature seems to be alive and dancing with love and laughter. Oh those crazy days of early love. Just the two of them are alone and on the center stage of time and the world. We hear her speaking--

2:8 - "The VOICE of my beloved"!

There is no other voice like his! It was a voice she knew, and loved, and expected. By the way, have you ever considered the fact that at the Rapture it is the VOICE of the Son of God that is heard? The Shout, the Voice, the Trump, all are His! "My sheep KNOW MY VOICE". He speaks and the sound of His voice...oh, it is comingled with love and truth and grace. Speak my Lord!

"Behold, he cometh LEAPING upon the mountains, SKIPPING upon the hills!"

What are mountains or hills, obstacles or distance, to him? He comes skipping! What has gotten into him? One gets the feeling that Solomon is as excited as she is! In our day it would be said that he bounds down the stairs, races through the front door, and peels rubber as he drives off to see his love. Smile when you say it, but time has not changed everything.

Now think on this. The Shulamite in her meditation is suddenly filled with anticipation. She remembers that her shepherd love has promised to return for her. She is impressed with the IMMINENCY of his return, that he may come at any moment. And by faith we hear the sound of His voice, and behold Him coming!

2:9 - "My beloved is like a roe or young hart."

This is an allusion to the speed with which he will return. She realizes that his love for her will brook no obstacle, nor will he tarry though mountains intervene. He will overcome them as the gazelle or young hart. And when our Lord comes, mountains or hills, or hell itself, will have no power to prevent that glorious appearing!

"Behold he standeth behind our wall, he looketh forth at the windows, shewing himself through the lattice."

"OUR WALL" seems to indicate a special trysting place for them. She thought she could see him standing there, then placing hands to his eyes to peer through the window. She just knew he could not wait to see her!

2:10 - "My beloved spake...Rise up my love...come away,"

She imagines he reaches in and takes her by the hand and practically pulls her outside, then says, "come away with me". He may have been gone for a time, but he had not changed his mind about her. He still loved her as before.

2:11-13 - Read these beautiful verses!

As you read remember the Shepherd lover's announced purpose in coming was to take her away to where he is (John 14:2-3). Forget the winter and the rain, for they are past. Springtime has arrived. What a wonderful background for love. The air is filled with the fragrance of flowers; the singing of birds is heard everywhere, and the skies are blue and smiling. Oh the feeling!

Have you ever wondered why Spring is the season for lovers? Surely it is because it reflects new life, freshness and happiness, and all takes on a grand new perspective. Black and white now turn to multicolor. Love can make an ordinary girl become attractive overnight! She walks with a glow on her face, a lilt to her head and with a skip in her step.

Love makes you want to communicate with the one you love. Nothing is unimportant. Every detail is like a souvenir keepsake for memory. Love produces a concern to know more about your lover.

"In our land"!

It is not enough that the bridegroom assures the bride of his undying love for her. Now he seeks to win her by telling of the beauties and joys of his own country to which he desires to take her. He even calls it OUR land!

Here again the Shulamite is like us. Our blessed Lover has told us of the beauties of His own country, and of His desire to have us "where He is". He probably senses in us a desire to remain in the barren land; where, like Lot, we have settled down. No wonder his appeal, "Come away...come away"! It is always love time in OUR land.

2:14 - "Let me see thy countenance, let me hear thy voice".

Love seeks a time and place. The couple in this song found a time and place to be together. While the prospects before them were glorious, he wanted to see her and hear her right now.

"My dove"!

What a lovely compliment he gives her in this title. A dove is comely and clean, gentle and guileless, and ever faithful (mating for life). For us who have fallen in love with the Great Shepherd, we gladly confess there is but "One Lord"!

"O my dove, that art in the clefts of the rock".

If no other passage in this delightful book would mark it of divine origin, this verse alone would do it. It speaks to us of our place of security in the Rock of Ages. Instantly our minds and hearts go to that One who was smitten for us. That cleft Rock has become both our shelter and security. Precious hiding place! He was wounded to provide for us a place of safety. He gently reminds us of this and, because we have flown to Him for refuge, and hidden ourselves in Him, He calls us His dove. The dove is utterly defenseless. Our only safety then is in His riven side.

While we are likened to a timid dove hiding in the cleft of a rock, we are not to hide ourselves from Him. So he reminds her of the secret access into his presence.

"The secret places of the stairs".

This speaks of the place of privilege. Love desires and must have response from its beloved. He reminds her of her privileged position as the favored one, and pleads for sight of her, or a word from her lips. And what they talk about is very important. We see that especially in the next picture.

VIII. Picture #8 reveals THE COST OF LOVE (2:15-17).

Let's not forget that Christ did not go to Calvary merely to save us from hell, or to populate heaven. He came to win a bride, a church, to Himself; a companion beloved for His own enjoyment throughout eternity; and so great is His value placed on our love that He pledges Himself to help us keep it.

As the love of Solomon and the Shulamite grows, it becomes more precious, and the greater its value becomes to them. It is so precious to them that they want more than anything else to protect and preserve it.

However a quietness, a moodiness, has set in upon the Shulamite. Solomon has not heard her voice for a while. He senses something is affecting their relationship. Wisely he speaks to her, identifies her problem as their problem, and resolves to work with her to protect their love against anything that would threaten or destroy it. With consummate grace he identifies himself with her.

2:15 - "Take us the foxes, the little foxes, that spoil the vines; for our vines have tender grapes".

They both realize this is a time calling for special care; for the grapes of their vines are reaching maturity. They realize there are some things that must be faced and talked out and settled before the wedding takes place; for courtship can be a most dangerous time. They decide to be alert and aware of anything that would ruin their relationship of love before God.

They decide to conduct a Fox Hunt! Be assured, as were they, that there are many little sly foxes that enter in to steal and destroy. Vineyard owners would make high walls and tight fences about their property to thwart anyone climbing over to steal the precious fruit. But the little foxes would dig under the wall or fence and devour the tender grapes.

Consider some of the destructive foxes that ruin the valuable vines. It may cost much to deal with them; but that is part of the high cost of loving. Our Lord said if we would follow Him we must first count the cost. We may have to destroy--

1. THE FOX OF UNCONTROLLED DESIRE.

What a sharp wedge this can drive between a couple. The one loved must be first in all considerations. Their needs and desires are foremost, not ours. "Love seeketh not her own"!

2. THE FOX OF UNREASONABLE MISTRUST.

Suspicion often creates the very thing it suspects! Jealousy and mistrust are sharp teeth that gnaw at the vines. "Love thinketh no evil". "Love suffereth long"!

3. THE FOX OF UNAPPRECIATED EFFORTS.

Recognize and honor the efforts of your spouse. It may be they need to work at love more than they speak of love. Acts, not words, are ties that bind.

4. THE FOX OF UNFEELING SELFISHNESS.

While selflessness will bond a marriage, selfishness will break it. One who lives for self, spends all on self, thinks only of self, may soon live by self! "Love vaunteth not itself"!

5. THE FOX OF UNFORGIVING ATTITUDE.

Love is quick to assume blame and to forgive. Love is also quick to receive forgiveness and ask no questions. An unforgiving spirit builds a wall that it cannot surmount. "Love rejoiceth in the truth"!

6. THE FOX OF UNCHECKED DISCONTENT.

Be content with such as you have. Never tolerate thoughts that the grass is greener on the other side of the fence. Fences have nothing to do with it. The grass is greener where it is watered! Keep the grass well watered! Never scratch the itch of wanderlust when mixed with discontent. Stabilize what you have and hold on with hope. Canoeing teaches us all, that when travelling the river, sitting still is essential to the journey.

7. THE FOX OF UNATTENDED LOVE.

The tender vines of love must be constantly ministered to. And it is imperative that both do their part in nurturing it. Love cannot go unattended!

"Take US the foxes."

Notice that Solomon does not say, "Let ME take the foxes, but rather, "LET US". Both must resolve and work together to protect and preserve the delicate vines of love.

Little foxes become big foxes! Therefore they must be recognized and dealt with while they can be handled. In the glow of romance some may be unseen, or even overlooked. They may be such foxes as differences of opinion, beliefs, or goals. But the difference may spell DANGER. Consider--

A. The Differences of TEMPERAMENT.

The spirit of one may always be merry, while the other is moody. One may have a positive attitude, while the other is negative. Is there compatibility or conflict in personalities? The one who leads before marriage will probably assume the role of leadership afterward.

B. The Differences of BACKGROUND.

Was the upbringing amid a large family setting, or a small one? Was the family background one of plenty, or poverty? Can they cope with living on little, or with a quiver full of children? Would they be able to put up with sharing the same tube of toothpaste, the same bed, bathroom, etc.

C. The Differences of VALUES.

What are their feelings about spiritual matters, the church, and serving God? What are their thoughts on children, discipline and home? Is there a oneness of mind on interests, standards, goals and values? The couple in the Song of Solomon were of one mind and accord in working together to deal with every destructive fox endangering their relationship. Being one in mind and work provided them a fulfilling experience of mutual companionship and belonging.

2:16 "My beloved is mine and I am his"!

The heart of the bride is singing again! She is thrilling at their oneness of mind and purpose. Her song finds expression in these beautiful words, "My beloved is mine and I am his". She can sing in spite of failure and foxes! How many times we have needed the loving touch of our Beloved to bring out the song of love again.

Oh the joy of togetherness in all things! And that joy of belonging was mutual. She could say, "We belong to each other; no part of us belongs to ourselves alone"!

That sense of mutual belonging to each other is imperative. The goal of the world is to discover "the perfect partner". The natural bent of mankind is to find the best looking, the most intelligent, the one with the greatest physique. But this verse reveals that love will not be found in the one who rates the highest by any set of standards, but in the one you know BELONGS to you!

Love does not look at another as a status symbol who will raise the level of prestige, but looks at the other as the counterpart, the one who completes you, the one with whom you can joyfully affirm your belongingness.

"He who feedeth (pastures) his flock among the lilies".

It is interesting that when the Shulamite affirms her mutual belongingness to Solomon, she reminds us who he is and draws attention to his SHEPHERD ROLE (one having the qualities of strength and gentleness). They seemed as opposites; he was strong and gentle, and she was as a frail flower. But they belonged to each other!

2:17 - "Until the day break, and the shadows flee away, turn, my beloved..."

Again she voices her longing for the wedding day when she will know his love fully, completely. And she is not crude or blunt when she says this. In a beautiful way she is asking Solomon to hurry and consummate their love in a wedding night that will last until morning....UNTIL the day break!

"Until"

The "until" times of Scripture deserve careful attention. This eighth picture then reveals the deep desire to protect their love, the confidence of belonging to each other, and the anticipation of fulfillment in marriage. By the way, are we crude to say that we love the Lord so much that we cannot stand being away from Him any longer? We want to see our love completed. We want also to protect that love until the day break.

"Be like a roe or a young hart upon the mountains of Bether".

Bether is translated "Separation". The Shulamite wants Solomon to shrink the miles that separate them by coming swiftly. Think of the cost of love for our Lord, for while we are apart, He is being robbed of great joy, the joy of our love for which He endured the Cross. "Come Lord Jesus."

IX. Picture #9 reveals THE CONCERN OF LOVE (3:1-5).

Did you notice the look of fear in the Shulamite's eyes? How did it get there? Well, fear will show up almost anytime something really important is about to take place in our lives. For example, just before a championship game, an athlete may lie awake all night thinking about all that might go wrong. What if sickness strikes, or he fails to perform as expected? Or he may want to win the contest so badly that his fear of losing increases. The Shulamite was having a dream of such proportions.

When a person dreams about failures, psychologists call them FEAR-FULFILLMENT DREAMS! Likewise, when one loves someone very much they dream of losing them. It is a Fear-fulfillment dream; or a dream in which one's fears are fulfilled!

The bride-to-be of this Song has just had such an experience. The wording given indicates the experience may be just a dream. If so, then she had a BAD dream! Whether or not a dream, it illustrates the intensity of her love for her husband-to-be. So deep is her love for him that the fear of losing him produces great anxiety.

3:1 - "**By night on my bed I sought him who my soul loveth**".

Four times in the first four verses she refers to her lover as "Him who my soul loveth". She is REACHING OUT to him from her innermost being; but she fears he is not there.

Why such feeling now? She had waited long times before, and it may be at this time it is but a day removed from the wedding. Why her sense of urgency and fear?

When lovers are together, time is timeless; and when they are apart, time is eternity. She wonders why he does not come. He promised he would. Had she been misled?

Love not only brings a greater experience of JOY, but a deeper capacity for PAIN as well. As the joy of her lover's presence became greater, so the sorrow of his absence became deeper. She loved him so much "it hurt!"

Because of her lover's long absence her heart has become perplexed and troubled. The Shulamite still loves him, but at this point she is not at all sure that he still loves her. Thus she dreams that she has lost him and cannot find him (as in Job 23:8-9).

How many of us, like David (Psalm 30:7), have had such an experience with our Lord. Sometimes He "withdraws" from us to test our love.

3:2 - "**I will rise...I will seek him...I sought him, but I found him not**".

The Shulamite could not wait until morning, so rises and goes to seek him. "I love him so much I cannot live with him!"

3:3 - "**The watchmen that go about the city found me; to whom I said...**"

The appeal to the "watchmen" of the city has its parallel in the flight of backslidden christians to unsaved psychiatrists, psychologists and hypnotists. They are the watchmen of the NIGHT! How wonderful that she "passed from them" (vs 4).

And when she passed from them SHE FOUND HIM!

3:4 - "I passed from them, BUT I FOUND HIM"!

Who was it she found? Oh, get this picture! The one she found was not the king from whose palace she had just come. The one she found was not the King, but her Shepherd! Would you believe that when the Shulamite left the palace to seek her shepherd lover, that Solomon was aware of her leaving! He must have quickly put on his shepherd garb and WENT TO SEEK HER! Is not that a shepherd for you! Oh how beautiful!

"I held him, and would not let him go!"

Oh the joy of having everything right with the one you love.

"Until I had brought him into my mother's house".

Had it been in her mind to go back to her mother? She must have been heading that way when Solomon, as the Shepherd, intercepted her. Home is always a good place to be. And who said mothers are not needed? Home and the heart rest better together, and "mother's house" is still a great place for comfort and counsel. SHE WAS A HOME GIRL! She loved her mother! So Solomon meets his mother-in-law.

3:5 - "I Charge ye..."

The song of love and joy is once again upon the lips of the bride. Her heart is at peace, and once more she voices the sound and Scriptural advice to be patient, and not encourage the emotions...but wait until he pleases (or until the proper time). She has rendered loves reasonable service (Rom. 12:1). She has chosen not to be conformed to the ways of the world, but to be wholly yielded to him.

That brings us to the long awaited moment, the wedding day. And the making of memories has no end.

Chapter Four

HERE COMES THE GROOM!

Mortal man is firmly bound by the feeble strands of sentimentality. Vain tradition and ceremony mark the milestones of his pilgrimage through this world. Pomp and Pageantry surround the triad of man's Birth, Marriage and Death. Natural man places great importance upon all three, for they all mark an entrance into a new life.

Marriage is indeed an entrance into a new life. Of course in this present day the wedding ceremony is anticlimactic because most couples has gone contrary to the revealed Word of God and are already living together. Therefore the wedding itself holds no great significance.

In the Song of Solomon marriage is held in sacred reverence. The two lovers placed such importance on marriage that they waited to give themselves to each other on that special day. The wedding then held all the significance and importance, joy and gladness, that God intended it to represent and reveal. It did begin a new life for them. Solomon, in telling of it, found himself singing. It was like a beautiful SONG to him.

Solomon now describes that glorious day of his gladness. We see in the distance the progression of royalty that begins it all. We behold the gala processional rolling into the city in verse six, but it is not until verse eleven that we understand it is a wedding processional. The king is coming, looking more glorious than ever, for it is the day of his espousal, the day of the gladness of his heart.

Here comes the Groom "crowned with the CROWN wherewith his mother crowned him"! Did you notice that both mothers played a great part in the character molding of this couple (vv 4, 11)? Solomon gives great honor to his mother, for he wears the crown of her making. What a timely tribute to Bathsheba. She was a woman who had done wrong, made her life right and produced for God a special man. Solomon loved his mother; he was not ashamed of her. She had graced his life with a kingly crown.

When the all-glorious King comes, He will be wearing many crowns (Rev. 19:12). Will one of those crowns upon His head be a crown of thorns? The crown wherewith His mother Israel crowned Him? What a day that will be when He comes.

In the verses before us all eyes focus on the Groom. The King is coming!

3:6 "Who is this that cometh out of the wilderness like pillars (clouds) of smoke, perfumed with myrrh and frankincense, with all powders...?"

The pillars of smoke are not clouds of dust rising from the feet of men and horses, or chariot wheels, but the burning of incense. Incense was customarily burned at the head of such processionals. Myrrh predominates here because Solomon knew the Shulamite was especially fond of the fragrance of myrrh (1:3). He did things to please her!

When our Lord comes He also will smell of myrrh (Psalm 45:9). Myrrh speaks of His sufferings, and we will always be reminded of those sufferings for us. It is remarkable that throughout eternity the Lord Jesus will be the only one who bears any mark of imperfection ("What are these wounds?" Zech. 13:6). We will ever be without spot or blemish, but He will bear the marks of Calvary.

But what mean these clouds of incense? Are they a picture of the CLOUDS in which the Bride shall be "caught up" to meet Him? Will the grand wedding processional be preceded by clouds of incense, perfumed with the fragrances of heaven?

3:7 - "Behold his bed..."

The word bed is best rendered "litter"; a canopied couch borne upon the shoulders of men by means of poles. In other words, Solomon comes for his bride in the car of state!

3:7b-8 - "Threescore valiant men are about it..."

Sixty mighty men of Israel have been selected as the King's attendants. This is a full dress military wedding! All of these men are expert warriors, picturing Solomon's ability to protect and provide for his bride.

Would you believe only one fellow stood up with me at our wedding. And he needed help to stand up for he was trembling with fear also. We could have used the support of sixty valiant men! As a pastor I have officiated at weddings where the groom had up to five attendants; but never sixty! These men were not there to keep Solomon from backing out! Sometimes the groomsmen are said to be there to make sure the groom does not turn chicken and head for the side door and freedom!

Sixty attendants fades into nothing in view of the coming of the King of Kings! When our Lord comes all the armies of heaven will attend Him (Rev. 19:11, 14).

3:7 - "Because of fear in the night"!

Rest assured of this, Solomon intended to see that his bride was brought to the palace in absolute safety. There are many enemies to make us fear in the night. When our Lord comes we shall be protected by the Holy Spirit, for we will travel awhile in enemy territory as we shall meet Him "in the air". Then soon shall come the morning, with night forever past.

3:9 - "A chariot of the wood of Lebanon".

Only the best was good enough for this wedding. This chariot was "fit for a king"!

3:10 - "He made the..."

Everything Solomon prepared was an expression of his love for the bride. And in this we find a wonderful picture of the One greater than Solomon. In the cedar wood of Lebanon we have our Lord's perfect humanity; fragrant and incorruptible. The silver speaks of His redemptive work, telling to all that He has redeemed us for Himself, and that we are His forever. The base of gold speaks of His divine righteousness, without which there could be no redemption for us. Its seat of royal purple speaks of His divine kingship; His right or reign. Beneath all, as if it were the reason for all this lavish display, is LOVE. "Paved with love"! His love is boundless. And what a perfect provision for our wilderness journey.

3:11 - "Go forth...behold King Solomon...in the day of his espousals..."

Here we know for certain that this is indeed a wedding procession, and the pomp and splendor were enough to dazzle any lady. Solomon had come to claim his bride!

"Behold King Solomon"! How often the Holy Spirit must prompt us to turn our eyes from the rich provision of our King, and behold Him as our Beloved! Think of Him in perfection of person and work, in the day of the gladness of His heart. What will it be like in that day when we behold our Shepherd as none other than our King! And what must the Shulamite girl have thought this day when the royal chariot stopped at her front door and the King stepped down; and, lo and behold, her fluttering heart recognized him at last as none other than her SHEPHERD LOVER! Did she promptly faint?

Will she now own her Shepherd also as her King? Of course she does and the wedding is on. The day of gladness is under way.

The Shepherd lover turned out to be the King, and the King became the Groom. Oh the day of the gladness of Solomon's heart.

Chapter Five

WHEN WEDDING BELLS RING

3:11 - "The day of the gladness of his heart".

Strangely enough the wedding of the King and Queen is not described. Only the wedding night is enlarged on in the next chapter, and we shall consider that.

The sole emphasis placed on the wedding ceremony is simply the meaning that it held for Solomon. The word "espousals" does not refer to the time of engagement, but to the wedding day. And the words "the crown wherewith his mother crowned him" lends to that thought, as though implying the symbolic act of approval and blessing of Bathsheba. And the blessing of mother is worth having!

The crown may also suggest victory. Solomon had needed the wise counsel of his mother in the affairs of heart. So Bathsheba placed a crown on Solomon's head something like that placed on a conqueror or athlete. He had conquered the heart of a wonderful woman. It was a day of victory and celebration. It was the day of the gladness of his heart, for finally that lovely virgin of the vineyard was his forever!

Call it "wedded bliss", or whatever good term applies, but GLADNESS is the word Solomon used to describe this moment. And it should be gladness from this time on for every couple. Consider a few verses of Scripture that reveal gladness to be God's design for marriage.

Ecclesiastes 9:9 - "Live joyfully with the wife whom thou lovest ALL THE DAYS OF THY LIVE...FOR THAT IS THY PORTION IN THIS LIFE"! Men, your wife is your "portion" in life! Make the best of that precious portion. Make her life happy... live joyfully with her ALL the days of your life. Husbands, this counsel is for you!

Many marriages would vastly improve if husbands realized that the wife God has given them is not only their portion in life, but also their blessing through which He intended to fill their heart and life with constant joy.

Proverbs 5:18 - "REJOICE with the wife of your youth"!! Again we see that God wants marriage to bring mutual happiness. Husband and wife are to rejoice together, but God explicitly taps the husband to make sure it happens.

Proverbs 12:4 - "An excellent wife is the CROWN of her husband"! A good woman will grace and crown the life of her husband. He may live without monetary things; but she is a treasure and he thus walks like a king.

Proverbs 18:22 - "He who finds a wife finds a good thing, and obtains FAVOR from the Lord"! A virtuous wife in a home is like a smile of God on a man. Could a man be anything less than GLAD with such a blessing? Men, be thankful to God for your portion.

A good wedding is like a special send off on life's journey. Weddings may appear beautiful, but often are deceiving. For after the wedding comes the MARRIAGE! What you wake up with may not be what was seen standing beside you at the church altar! Fantasy becomes reality! Flowers turn into hair curlers, bad breath and kids! The bride does not thereafter wear a flowing gown around the house, nor does the groom wear a tuxedo to work.

Someone has said, "Weddings are beautiful, it is what comes afterward that is ugly." It need not be that way. Weddings are usually thought of as fairytale times when Real Life is suspended. "And they lived happily ever after" seems impossible, if only for a day. To read children bedtime stories with happy endings will inevitably find one of them asking, "And THEN what happened?"

Would that be applicable to you? Has something happened that mars the memory of your wedding day? Does the very thought of that marital moment bring joy and gladness to your heart, or do you wish to high heaven it had never taken place? Has the sweet milk of marriage turned sour? Have you succumbed to the situation and look upon life and marriage as a monumental irrelevance?

Hope extends loving hands to you. Despite the ups and downs of life, marriage can work and be wonderful. God has so designed it. The sound of wedding bells can linger in the air. Once again the happiness you knew on that day can pervade your heart and home, continue on and even increase. Believe it, marriage truly can get better and better.

Let no one come to the wedding day with doubts goading the mind and conscience as to their life's partner. Marriage is too intimate a relationship for a couple to get started wrong. Together they will walk the rugged roads of life. Together they will share the countless tears and trials that come as surely as sparks fly upward. As a marital team they two must walk and work as one. Let not one be spiritual and the other unspiritual. Let not one be industrious and the other indolent. Let not one be live-wire and the other dead-pan. Let them not be an un-matched team. That thought of marriage most certainly passed through the mind of God when He wrote that Israel was not to hitch an ox and an ass together!

Frankness at times becomes the most reasonable policy. Therefore let it be said that from this point on in our study the frying pan may get too hot to handle. Which simply means you may decide to cool it! The heat may be more than you can stand. It may be you will choose not to face what lies ahead in Solomon's Song.

Assuming your decision is to endure the heat let us move on to the fourth chapter of the Song of Solomon, where we will bug the honeymooner's bridal suite!

Kindly accept another warning, and beware! From here on you might get hurt! What is said may go contrary to your thinking! Proceed with utmost caution, for it will be like walking through a mine field!

Chapter Six

HONEY IN THE HONEYMOON

The wedding ceremony has now taken place, the hubbub of the reception is over, and the honored guests have all gone their way. The happy couple is headed down the road with tin cans rattling behind the souped-up chariot. Solomon has carried his bride across the threshold of the bridal suite at the Conrad Hilton in Jerusalem, and they are laughing. She suddenly becomes shy. Perhaps that fleeting look on her face is due to the little fear that has appeared and registered on the horizon of her heart. Will this man who courted her, and spoke so romantically to her during those wonderful days, be the tender, loving husband that she had expected him to be?

Solomon must have sensed her need for reassurance. He is the first to speak.

4:1 - "Thou art fair, my love..."

Solomon's opening words indicate what every marriage needs; a husband who is lost in the loveliness of his wife. Of course it is when we are entirely occupied with our Beloved that we are the most pleasing to Him. Solomon proceeds to eloquently describe her physically. Through this we learn a little of what we mean to Christ. His great love for us comes into focus.

Paul speaks of the Bride as Christ's BODY! How beautiful the Church must look to Him. To the pursuer of pornography these verses must seem foolish, but in Solomon's description there is nothing obscene or vulgar, indecent or course; for LOVE DOTH NOT BEHAVE ITSELF UNSEEMLY..... THINKETH NO EVIL (I Cor. 13:5). All here is in keeping with the ho-

47

liness of this Book We are standing on Holy Ground!

The wife's body is beautiful, not because it represents a sexual object to be used or abused, but because God created it to house her personality with all its feeling, understanding and responses. SEPARATING A PHYSICAL BODY FROM THE PERSON INSIDE HAS SERIOUS AFFECTS UPON THE SELF-WORTH OF THAT INDIVIDUAL. To treat someone like a "thing", or tool, damages their sense of dignity and self respect.

Remember, the Shulamite had asked him to "be like the roe" or GAZELLE (2:17). She had hoped for a gentle Gazelle! Husbands, what are you? A GORILLA, or a GAZELLE? It would do you well to ponder that.

Solomon, of course, is gracious and gentle, and he gives seven aspects of her beauty. He was telling her that she was absolutely perfect to him!

"Thou hast dove's eyes"!

Did you realize that the Shulamite says the same thing of Solomon (5:12)? A wife and husband should be able to look into each other's eyes and see the same love and loyalty. Too many have lost their doves' eyes!

Looking into each other's eyes is very romantic. Anyone is a fool if they think it is foolish! The eyes tell so much. Solomon saw in those eyes her deep love for him. When we look into the eyes of our lovely Lord all tears will forever cease as we will be looking into eyes that glow with love for us. We are told one cannot cry while looking into the eyes of one who truly loves them!

Dove's eyes are pure (they seek no carrion; as at the Ark) . Dove's eyes are far-seeing (discerning. Faith sees). Dove's eyes are gentle (not fierce, or dull).

Solomon knew his wife must feel good about herself, so he builds her self esteem. For him to have said that her eyes were as Crows' eyes, or Hawks' eyes, would have brought instant re-percussions. A man might say to his love that her eyes were like POOLS, and mean cesspools! Later Solomon did speak of her eyes as the "POOLS of Hesbon" (7:14). Her eyes were peaceful and restful.

They BOTH had Doves' eyes! They both had the same mind! They thought alike! And that is very important in a marriage.

Eyes reveal the personality of the soul. They are the windows that let us see what the inner person is really like. The fact that it says DOVES' EYES seems to indicate her Godliness! God's Spirit dwelt in her! She was some kind of woman. We would say she was like Christ. The Spirit of God is likened to a Dove.

> The Dove is the only bird that can drink with its head down (suggests HUMILITY).
> The Dove is the only bird without a GALL (suggests lack of bitterness or guile).
> The Dove is the only bird with a great sense of direction (it will find its way home though thousands of miles away). The believer too can sense God's will, and will keep moving toward heaven and home.
> The Dove has eyes that DILATE at the sight of their mate. And they MOURN when absent from them.

"Dove's eyes within thy locks"!

It appears that Solomon is holding her in his arms, and they are looking into each other's eyes; and her hair keeps getting in the way! Some think the word "locks" means she was VEILED (as was the custom of women). But it seems rather awkward to believe she would remain veiled on her wedding night". The veil was to seal her off from the eyes of other men, not from her husband. Solomon goes on to describe her, and how could he do so if she were veiled? No, the locks refer to her hair! She probably had the old Veronica Lake style that closed off one eye. But mark it down, she had fixed up her hair for him! He speaks of it.

"Thy hair is as a flock of goats..."

What in the world does Solomon mean by this? Is he trying to undo everything by insulting his bride on their wedding night? How unflattering it sounds to be told your hair looks like a flock of goats! If a modern husband said that to his wife on their wedding night, or at any time, he would be met with either tears or a frying pan. Was Solomon cruel?

The Shulamite well understood how his shepherd mind saw this. He envisioned the end of a long day and the goats descending from Mount Gilead. The members of the flock blend in to form a dark stream flowing smoothly down the mountain into the valley, and the sun just cresting the top puts a sparkle on their wool. Her hair was like a dark stream flowing smoothly downward. She had long dark flowing hair! She must have been a brunette!

There is nothing more attractive, more hypnotic to a man, than a woman's hair. It is her glory!

"That appear from Mount Gilead".

The word "appear" means "to leap playfully down"! Solomon saw her hair as it gracefully tumbled down over her shoulders, and he was held captive by it.

4:2 - "Thy teeth are like a flock of newly shorn sheep... come up from washing"!

Her teeth are beautiful! When she smiled it got to Solomon. He said her teeth reminded him of little lambs scurrying out of the water...playful...teasing...making him smile just to watch them. Her smile caused him to smile in return.

"From washing".

She kept her mouth CLEAN! (She may have used Colgate).

"Every one beareth twins".

Her uppers and lowers matched! Her teeth were not like stars which come out at night!

"None is barren among them"

The bride still had all her teeth! Not a tooth was missing! When she grinned there were no toothless gaps!

4:3 - "Thy LIPS are like a thread of scarlet".

Solomon describes her lips as scarlet. Apparently she used lipstick! Do you suppose she chose strawberry flavor? At any rate she used some type of cosmetic in a comely way to highlight her natural beauty.

"Like a thread"!

This is an indication of their delicateness! To have said her lips looked like a hay rope would have suggested a big mouth. This lady was no blabber mouth, no gossiper, She was dainty, delicate, discreet.

"Scarlet".

While this could obviously mean that she was in good health, it would seem to imply that her speech was comely; like the speech of a child of God should be. She was spiritually healthy, and her WORDS proved it!

"Thy temples are like a piece of a pomegranate within thy locks".

Solomon may have had her blushing by this time. The pomegranate has a red and white skin, so the word "temples" could refer to her cheeks. Those soft sides of her face are now red. She is healthy and flushed with beauty and excitement.

Temples are often spoken of as the seat of thought. So the "pomegranate" becomes the key here, as the inner part of the fruit is filled with good meat and seeds. Thus Solomon sees her as SWEET IN HER INNER CHARACTER AND PRODUCTIVE IN HER THOUGHTS.

4:4 - "Thy neck is like the tower of David..."

A tower is straight and tall. It is not bowed, as in a yoke. Solomon is not suggesting that she looked like a Giraffe! Rather he is intimating that she walked erect, queenly! She showed great grace and character. She was stately, manifesting dignity, character, and gracefulness.

"Builded for an armoury, whereon there hangs a thousand bucklers, all shields of mighty men".

David must have built a museum (II Kings 11:10) in which he displayed the weapons of his mighty men as memorials of victory. Perhaps he displayed the spears of Adino, Eleazer, Beneniah, etc. Likewise the Church acts as a memorial to Jesus Christ: "This do in REMEMBRANCE..." The Shulamite was more than a conqueror through him that loved her! She was some trophy of his grace!

Solomon is letting us know that this woman had a lot to her; she was no easy "pushover". She had a mind of her own and feelings to be respected and understood. She was not committing herself as a slave to Solomon's every wish. She was not going to be a doormat for anyone to walk on. She had integrity and strength, and Solomon admired those qualities in her.

Solomon's bride was a source of strength to him. He found in her his strength, his comfort, and his encouragement.

"Shields"!

Because Solomon is thinking of her neck, it appears that the "shields" refer to the ornaments (jewels, etc.) that normally adorned her as she walked in public. He was always proud of her!

4:5 - "Thy two breasts are like two young roes that are twins..."

Remember we are on holy ground, and "marriage is honorable in all" (Heb. 13:5). But some who read these words conclude otherwise. It is said that the Jews forbade the reading of this Song until the age of thirty! However this is chaste language. Sin has robbed us of the capacity to look at things right.

This is the SEVENTH aspect of Solomon's description of his bride. The "breasts" speak of her Womanhood, her capacity for Motherhood, her ability to satisfy little ones with comfort and life giving sustenance.

Solomon is saying, "YOU ARE PERFECT FOR ME"! In all reverence we can say that God is endorsing their lovemaking! Solomon describes her breasts as two little fawns. He longed to gently touch and caress them. God made them that way to satisfy a man. And a husband's desires are to be satisfied by his wife's breasts and not by those of someone else! Solomon makes that clear in Proverbs 5:19-20; "let her breasts satisfy thee at all times; and be thou RAVISHED (intoxicated) always with her love". ALL TIMES AND ALWAYS! No man need to be looking around, he has more than enough at home to satisfy him. And what God saith is true!

God calls marriage a wonderful relationship. "Marriage is honorable in all". It is high and holy and not to be treated as something unclean. Now notice the other side of that picture "but whoremongers and adulterers God will judge" (Hebrews 13:4).

Solomon has just presented us a seven-fold description of his bride. To him she was super special! God is giving wives an insight into the fact that they have great ability to AFFECT THE HEART of their husbands! A wife affects her husband both physically and emotionally. May she never forget that, and may she use those endowments and abilities wisely and prayerfully.

4:6 - Until the day break..."

Those breasts that had carried the sachet of myrrh and frankincense were now his. Love was now complete and fulfilled.

Notice that Solomon is always sensitive to his wife to make her feel special to him and secure in his love. How well this is seen in his next words.

4:7 - "Thou art fair, my love, there is NO SPOT in thee"!

Solomon did not mention her appendectomy scar, or the wart on her back, or the birth mark on her shoulder. He did not hint that she should work on an ugly roll of fat. He told her she was WITHOUT FAULT! She was just right for him!

"No spot in thee"!

These are the words used of sacrificial animals acceptable for worship (I Pet. 1:19). Our Lord was "without spot or blemish". The Church also is seen "without SPOT or wrinkle, or any such thing" (Eph. 5:27). Solomon is emphasizing her purity! She has offered herself without spot to him...AND HE WORSHIPS HER (like Christ loved the Church)! Love is an offering! And she gives herself, for love gives.

In this day of easy sex and numerous affairs, folks have lost sight of the value of virginity. The truth of this Song is that if ones desires the maximum amount of happiness all the days of their life, then the best way to assure that is to remain a virgin until married! The memory of purity will crown your life.

Think deeply here, for Solomon is telling us that a husband's desire for the love of his wife involves four things:

1. Being ALONE with her (4:8).
2. Being AROUSED by her (4:9).
3. Being ATTRACTED by her lovemaking (4:10).
4. Being AFFECTED by her sweetness and smell (4:11).

Let us consider these four aspects.

BEING ALONE

4:8 - "Come with me from Lebanon ... to Amana ... Shenir ... Hermon.." etc.!

Solomon planned a surprise trip! Husbands, take note of that! Solomon says he will take her for a trip back to her home country which she loves. He describes where they will go and what they will do and see...just the two of them. They will journey down from the summit of Amana, one of the outermost peaks of the Lebanon mountains. They will visit Shenir and Hermon. It appears Solomon had built a royal get-a-way residence in this region; it was his San Clemente and Camp David. Something like a northern White House. He would deliver her from the dangers of lions and leopards.

Our Lord also calls us to higher ground; to mountain top experiences with Him. We are to "seek those things which are above...where Christ is".

Solomon was not only a wise man, it appears he was somewhat of a mind reader. He realizes what his bride has gone through in a relatively short time. Hardly any time has passed since she had been walking barefoot in the vineyards, then was whisked off to the palace at the request of the king; then involved in a gala wedding procession, then married to the richest man in the world, who also is the King, and now finding herself ALONE with him in a bridal suite! That is quite a lot to happen to a country girl in so short a period of time!

The Shulamite bride probably feels a little out of place.

She is tense and nervous. There comes over her again the feeling of worthlessness. She may be thinking more of home than of him. So here in verse eight Solomon deals with her first concern; a touch of homesickness for Lebanon. He suggests that they go there on a trip.

The second problem Solomon dealt with was her sense of worthlessness. That is why he spends the first seven verses telling her how beautiful she is. He is very sensitive to his wife's psychological and emotional feelings and concerns, and places her needs above the satisfaction of his own physical needs!

Every woman needs to feel her husband wants to make love to her as a PERSON, not as a BODY! Or a "thing"! Too many men never take time to praise their wife, or tell her what she means to them. Instead they take a "thirty-second" approach into the bedroom, then wonder why their wife never seems responsive! If your love-making tends to last only five to ten minutes, you might consider whether you are really making love to your wife as a person! Perhaps you are more concerned about yourself than about her.

Without doubt it is difficult to find time to be alone. Some tend to avoid such times. But a healthy marriage will see a couple finding time to be alone. Husbands, there is a high cost to loving. Perhaps a trip should be planned for just the two of you. Take a couple of days away in some motel, away from the distractions of home. It will cost, but take time out to let her know you want to be alone with just her.

"Look from the top"!

Solomon is quaintly saying, "Let us put the world beneath us!"

BEING AROUSED

4:9 - "Thou has ravished my heart..."!

Solomon is letting her know that she has his old ticker pumping fast! He is saying that she makes his blood rush through his heart. In this he is praising her for the way she affects him!

"My sister...my spouse".

In their culture "sister" was an affectionate term for one's wife.

"Thou has ravished my heart with one of thine eyes...".

Her eyes were not only alluring, but arousing. Just ONE eye did it! Now don't say she was not trying to make him want her.

"With one link of your necklace".

The necklace worn on her wedding night seemed to capture her beauty and accentuate it. She may have been a "natural beauty", but she took time to make herself more attractive for Solomon. There is no merit in refusing to look attractive. What do you do to RAVISH your husband's heart? To make him desire you? Slopping around the house in sagging sweat pants is no boon to beauty. With a little help in the Personal Looks Department, it might be amazing to see how the old boy would come alive!

BEING ATTRACTED

4:10 - "How fair is thy love...much better is thy love...THAN ALL..."!

Love is the exquisite chord that binds all things together in a melody of sweetest harmony. And this wife did not have a passive love! Solomon commends her on how responsive she is. When a wife asks whether she should be aggressive in lovemaking, one wonders if she has read the Song of Solomon. Twice here Solomon mentions his bride's love, or lovemaking.

"The smell of thine ointments..."

She smelled good! Many wives and husbands should take time to smell better. Many do not even brush their teeth! Oh the bad breath one runs up against. Like one man was overheard to comment, when being introduced to someone, "I don't remember your face, but I sure recognize your breath!" There is nothing attractive about not smelling good.

BEING AFFECTED

4:11 - "Thy lips...drop as the honeycomb ..."

Solomon even praises her for her remarkable kisses. Sweet they were, like honey! Does that sound like she was unresponsive? Wives have great capability to affect the heart of their husband. The capability should be wisely considered. No man, or woman, is motivated by unkind words, unkempt appearance, unpleasant smells, or unwarranted withdrawal.

In all likelihood you did not marry a Solomon. And it is true the husband must respond to God's love as well as his wife's, but it must be understood that the wife can have great impact in affecting his heart and desires.

"Thy garments"!

We have no way of knowing what she wore on that wedding night, but you can bet she did not come to Solomon wearing two pairs of flannel pajamas and three housecoats! She apparently wore see-through lingerie, for Solomon was able to describe her body through it. Some seem to believe they are living in a nunnery!

The thought of her garments might well prompt us to camp awhile and think again on the matter of appearance. Do we dress up for our spouse? Now we know that God looks on the heart, but man has a habit of looking on the outward appearance. Does that MRS before your name stand for Miserable Rut of Sloppiness? Or does that MR before your name suggest More Rummage? A look at some folks gives you that immediate impression.

Visit a supermarket and nine out of ten women pushing carts look like survivors of a shipwreck. They spend more time squeezing tomatoes and cabbage heads than selecting a good shade of lipstick. And it does not end there. The aisles of the average store reveal a potpourri of feminine ugliness. Women of all ages seem bent on looking like Girl Scouts just home from a month's camping trip.

To set the record straight, men are no less guilty of sloppiness than many women. Too often men lay around the house in grimy sweatshirts or dirty work clothes. They lounge in front of the TV and watch football with extra large bellies hanging over their belts, loudly burping, and wondering why their wives are not more sexually responsive to them.

How strange that husbands and wives often save their best for comparative strangers while their mate has to settle for what they can get. We speak kindly to others, but growl at our mates. We smile at others but glare at our spouse. Company may come and we exhibit utmost graciousness and become ultimate conversationalists, but retreat into silence when alone.

It does not take a mint to look and smell good. Every man needs a magnet that keeps drawing him back home. There are hundreds of magnets out there in the work-a-day world, but make your magnet the most powerful!

Now no woman should be expected to appear as if she just stepped out of a beauty parlor twenty-four hours a day. Her home should be a place where she can relax and "let her hair down". All we are suggesting is that often too much hair is let down and the result reveals thoughtlessness toward our other half; and we become a turn-off instead of a turn-on.

Husbands, the greater responsibility lays upon you! Do you make your wife feel loved and needed? Solomon did! Look how he praised her in the verses of this chapter. Every wife needs to hear things like that from her husband. It is imperative that she know she is loved and needed! Just like you need to be loved and needed. If your boss continually made you feel unnecessary to the function of the company, your motivations to do a good job would rapidly diminish. Likewise the home is the work-world of the wife. She needs to know she is succeeding at "her job", just as much as the husband needs to know he is doing his work well.

The problem is the wife often has difficulty trying to determine exactly what she is needed for. She may feel her routine is a drudgery of keeping the house clean, the meals fixed, the family washing done, and satisfying her husband in bed. She may not mind that, but she needs to know how much she is appreciated for it. She needs to hear her husband's praise and encouragement. It gives her the needed incentive to go on. Every husband should let his wife know what her faithful support means to him, how it gives him satisfaction and strength. He must praise her for believing in him, relying on him, and trusting in him. She needs to know her husband recognizes the vital and important part she plays in his life and home; that he relies on her and could not do without her.

President Gerald Ford, in his acceptance speech, said, "I am indebted to no man and to only one woman"! He was telling the world that his wife had contributed to his success. He was giving her due honor (I Pet. 3:7).

Men must also understand that woman are incurable romantics with no discernible interest in ever being cured! Chances are the wife still has stashed away every one of her husband's old love letters. Men are guilty of not recognizing the importance of romance to her. If a man has thwarted romance he generally throws himself into work and finds fulfillment there. Not so with a woman. She FEELS the lack more deeply.

Your wife may keep those old love letters because they are so dumb, yet so wonderful. Romance embraces both aspects. Women are thrilled with the unlikely and unexpected. They enjoy the craziness of love. Do something for your wife as impractical as writing a dumb letter, like you used to. She will cherish it When I was a boy, I used to buy my mother the dumbest gifts, and she loved every one of them! Buy your wife some special things too. Get her some choice perfume, scented soap, a basket of fruit, or a new outfit she wanted and knew you could not afford. But get out of your rut!

The only difference between a rut and a grave is the depth

of it! The Routine Rut can be devastating. Do something to get out of it, even if what you do is dumb and crazy. Let sex go! Work together on making an apple pie at midnight! Phone her from work and call her "beautiful"! Take a mystery trip. Do a lot of laughing together. Laughter not only has curative qualities, but enduring qualities. Remember he who laughs, lasts! Also remember "thy garments". Look the part of a husband and wife team who think of each other. And always smell good! Make memories!

4:12 - "A garden enclosed is my spouse ..a spring shut up..a fountain sealed"!

Solomon is praising his bride for keeping herself pure. In three brief descriptions he sets forth the declaration of her virginity.

That garden which had been enclosed, shut up, and sealed, is now his. She has removed the locks and taken down the barriers, and says to Solomon, "I am all thine". What joy must have been hers to come thus to her husband on their wedding night.

Solomon gives needy counsel regarding premarital and extramarital sex. In Proverbs 5:15-20 he issues words of warning. Read it! "Drink waters out of thine OWN cistern...out of thine OWN well" (or from your own spouse)!

"A garden enclosed"!

The bride has allowed no trespassing in her garden. Her body remained off-limits to any but the one she married.

"A spring SHUT UP...a fountain SEALED"!

A fountain, or well, was often sealed to protect against possible impurity getting in. None could remove water from the well except the rightful owner. The Holy Spirit also seals believers to keep out defilement. Solomon viewed his pure bride as:

A GARDEN - for Fruitfulness!

A SPRING - for Freshness!

A FOUNTAIN - for Fullness!

4:13-15 - Reading these verses brings an awareness of Solomon's complete satisfaction with his bride. He is saying, "She is everything to me"!

4:15 - "A fountain of gardens..."

One almost feels this should read, "A garden of FOUNTAINS!" But Solomon, like our Lord, sees his bride as a living fountain; and from that fountain come GARDENS!

"A Fountain...a Well...and Streams!"

Solomon is saying that his bride's responses to him are like "living waters", and as the delicious tasting "streams of Lebanon". How refreshing they were to him. The couple enjoyed each other and were quick to let each other know it. Solomon told her it was just like being in paradise to be with her.

Understanding the Song of Solomon correctly brings the realization that married couples are to mutually experience sexual pleasure. That means that husbands are to be sensitive and loving in their understanding and approach to their wives and their sexual needs; and vice versa.

Read I Cor. 7:3 - "Let the husband render to his wife the affection DUE her (she has that right), and likewise the wife to her husband" (he has that right)! Sex in marriage is not to be one-sided! The Scripture teaches that BOTH husband and wife own the responsibility to minister to each other!

Without doubt many wives are convinced their husbands are animalistic, thinking only of themselves in the matter of sex. Their desires never relate to a communication of love. Too many have come to believe sex is something to be endured instead of enjoyed. How contrary to God's intention.

4:16 - "Awake, O north wind, and come...thou south... blow upon my garden, that... "

Did you notice anything different in these words? Previously the Shulamite had given the admonishment, "Do not awaken my love" (2:7, 3:5). Now she says, "AWAKE"! The prohibitions so necessary prior to marriage are now done away.

The Shulamite is now responding, and invites her husband to come to his garden. In the last of the verse she bids him to "Eat his pleasant fruits"! She realizes that she is HIS garden; and wants him to satisfy himself with her.

Rest assured there is not a husband on earth who would refuse such an invitation coming from a wife so deeply committed to enhancing their love relationship.

The Shulamite is saying they will keep on loving each other though the north wind (adversity), or the south wind (prosperity) blow upon them. Let come what will, their love shall endure. The north wind may remove the clouds from their skies, or the south wind might bring storm and rain, but regardless she was committed to him for all of time.

5:1 "I am come into my garden..."

How could a husband be distant after that? Note the mutual acceptance worded here. All things blend together in that little word "MY".

"MY myrrh and MY spice."

"MY honeycomb with MY honey."

"MY wine with MY milk."

These combinations reveal their mutual enjoyment of each other, and their giving what is due the other. Their lives and loves blend, and that is the way it should be. It meant honey in the honeymoon, and would mean music in the marriage.

5:1c - "Eat O friends, yea drink abundantly, O beloved"!

Who is this speaking? Some suggest that the wedding guests have returned (as for an old time horning!) Not so, for while this Book gives no mention of the name of God, it surely must be His voice that is heard! How intimately God is involved in our affairs! Thus their Creator, the most concerned wedding guest of all, the One who prepared them for this night of His design, lifts His voice and gives pleased approval. God endorses the love and the lovemaking of this couple who kept themselves pure in His sight. He takes pleasure in them, and in their marriage.

Few experience this kind of wedding night. Few know the sense of God's approval on their wedding and loving. Perhaps it is because the courtship did not prepare them rightly. This couple experienced a beautiful wedding night because they had kept themselves for each other by a right courtship.

How wonderful it would be to say that Solomon and his bride lived happily ever after. It was not to be so recorded. Into every life some rain must fall. What garden is there that does not need the blessing of rain to make it what it ought to be? What rose has never felt the wetness of raindrops on soft petals? And it is true that tears often wash the eyes and cheeks of the Bride, and Bridegroom, even after the wedding is over. It is true in this case. The Song of Solomon is a very realistic Book. God knows!

While this love story is a PATTERN of romance for others to follow, it also presents the PROBLEMS of marriage, and the PRINCIPLES for solving them.

With that in mind let us proceed.

Chapter Seven

THE SACRED TRUST

5:1 "MY garden, MY sister, MY spouse, MY honeycomb, MY milk"!

Let every man who would have wisdom, and know God's blessing on his marriage, ponder this five-fold trust! The taking of a wife is no trivial matter. To Solomon the sweet Shulamite was his garden to be tended, his sister to be protected, his spouse to be loved, his honeycomb to be enjoyed, and his milk to be desired. She was to ever be delighted in, never discarded.

Solomon reveals a growing awareness of his responsibilities as a husband. The realization of the responsibilities that go with just knowing what God expects of us as a man is appalling, but it is enough to scare the living daylights out of any man to become aware of what God expects of him as a husband!

Solomon records the words of God's approval in the closing of this verse. Notice that the benediction of blessing on their marriage comes only AFTER Solomon has acknowledged the five-fold "MY" of sole responsibility. He is conscious of the fact that God is watching their home and love. How serious then must be the discharging of that sacred trust before God.

The home is of such importance to God that when Adam and Eve were driven from the garden, He allowed them to take the best part of paradise with them. The home was all that came intact out of the fall. God in His mercy retained for man the blessings of marriage, love and home. God intends that every home be a part of paradise, a refuge from this sin-cursed world. And upon fallen man was thrust the responsibility to head that home and hold it together.

Every man must realize that God has placed upon him duties and responsibilities and burdens that women are not fitted to carry, required to carry, nor intended to carry. Did you know:

1. God commanded the MAN not to eat of the tree of life! (Gen. 2:16- 17).

2. When the Edenic couple sinned, it was MAN that God sought out. "Adam, where art thou?" (Gen. 3:9).

3. Though the woman sinned first, it was MAN that God reproached; for Adam was responsible for his wife! (Gen. 3:17a).

4. It was to MAN God said, "Cursed be the ground for THY sake." (Gen. 3:17b). Not that Eve had no blame in the matter, but that Adam bore responsibility.

5. It was to MAN that God said, "In the sweat of THY face shalt thou eat bread..." (Gen. 3:19). Adam was clearly to be held accountable to provide for his wife.

6. As MEN we are held responsible and accountable for our wives and families, whether we desire to be or not!

7. Furthermore, it is to MAN God issued the all-comprehensive command to love. The believing husband is to exemplify before his wife the same selflessness, submission, and sacrifice with which Christ loved the Church. In the contextual continuance of Eph 5:19- 25, the husband is commanded to first be filled with the Spirit and then to be Christ-like in loving the wife God entrusted him with. And it appears no man is truly Spirit-filled who does not so love his wife and live for her.

Man's portion before the Almighty is absolutely awesome!! Every man who marries must understand that, before God, he has assumed a responsibility that is a sacred trust! What a moment that was when God GAVE Eve to Adam! God "brought her unto the man" (Gen. 2:22)! In other words God led, or conducted, Eve to Adam and presented her to him as in a wedding ceremony. That act implied the formal and solemn bestowment of Eve to Adam in the bonds of the marriage covenant. WHEN

ADAM ACCEPTED EVE AS HIS WIFE HE AUTOMATICALLY ASSUMED THAT SACRED TRUST! Eve therewith belonged to Adam, and like our Lord he became responsible to be the Saviour and Protector of that body! Years of experience as a pastor and counselor have given reason to believe that at least seventy-five percent of the fault in marriage lies with the husband. Man fails as head and spiritual leader! God performed the marriage ceremony and placed man as Head of the home, and since that time no marriage has been successful where, that Headship has been abdicated and God's plan discarded.

Where a man disobeys God in duty and leadership as Head of the home, and where a wife refuses to accept that Headship and usurps the authority which God forbade her, sin and chaos reign. And where sin and chaos reign, heartache and trouble abound.

Adam was placed in the position of headship before Eve was created. Eve was not created as an equal partner, but as a helpmeet. Like an assistant under Adam's oversight and tutelage. He was the Head, and she was the Helpmeet. Let it be made clear, however, that though Eve was created second does not mean she was inferior! That she was taken from Adam's side does not suggest she was a side issue! In no way was woman created as an afterthought by God; like something thrown in to provide balance. God did as he did to establish the fact that man is Head, and therefore he bears the responsibility. God made it plain to Eve that her husband was to be the Head, and that all her desire was to be toward him (Gen. 3:16c). Adam had the responsibility to rule. And any man not willing to assume that sacred responsibility should never get married!

True, man is made of dust and proves frail and faulty. Therefore there will be problems. But by submitting to God's Word, and to one another before God, every husband and wife will find that any difficulty that arises may be dealt with. Life can be a heavenly harmony. There can be the sound of music in marriage.

Chapter Eight

DEALING WITH DIFFICULTIES

Who has not heard of blue Mondays and rainy days? They occur in every life and marriage. Even in the life of a King and Queen! There is no way of knowing just how long the honeymoon happiness lasted, but the star struck couple probably believed it would go on forever. We can only guess when their first problem came, but it did come. In fact it is the next significant event recorded in Solomon's Song. Perhaps they especially remembered it because they did not expect such a thing could happen; and surprises are hard to forget.

Solomon had grown accustomed to the willing response of love. Yet there came a time when he was met with cold indifference from his wife. It signaled a break in their marital progress. What could be worse than to have your sincere expression of love met with a yawn? Or met with a sharp, "Just what did you mean by that?"

The first problem appeared when the Shulamite did not feel like sexually responding to him. No matter what the reasoning may be for such response, hurt feelings or anger usually result.

There are times with anyone when they may just not feel up to love-making, so there must be an understanding on the part of both. It also must be remembered that we have declared ourselves COMMITTED to our spouse. Their feelings and needs are priority.

Some misunderstanding husband might complain, "Why does my wife have so many headaches at bedtime?" An unresponsive wife might say, "Well, he has another thought coming if he wants to make love to me! He had better start helping around the house, and doing his part with the kids!" Of course it works both ways.

There are so many variables where we can hurt the other, and quench the fire of love. Just how do you react to overtures for love making from your spouse? Do you reckon it an opportunity to return love? Or is the love making all one sided? Like one man said, "When we make love my wife reads a book, or chews gum!" He was hurt by indifference.

How do you convey your feelings, or indifference? When bed time rolls around do you announce that you are going to stay up a little longer and read a book? Perhaps you even sleep in another room because they snore too loud! No matter how one justifies indifference, the spouse is left with a hurt. Let us consider the bride's apathy seen here.

5:2 - "I was asleep, but my heart was awake..."

It happened again! The Shulamite was having another bad dream. Remember that dreams are often the result of the way we have been living or thinking. People have a serious biological need to dream. It is one way nature deals with stress. Perhaps the bride has been dealing with stress, for she seems to be having bad dreams often. Like in 3:1, "By night..." Night is plural and suggests something recurring. We would say, "night after night"! Apparently she kept dreaming bad dreams. Something was building up. And the point of her dream revealed a growing reluctance on her part!

"It is the voice of my beloved... saying, 'Open for me .. my love'"!

She dreams of her husband coming home late from work and wanting to make love after she had already bathed and gone to bed. She understands he has been thinking of getting home to be with her, and nowhere else in the Song does Solomon speak in such affectionate terms; "MY LOVE, MY DOVE, MY UNDEFILED!" In her dreams she knows he is full of love for her.

"It is the voice of my beloved that knocketh."

Does not that sound like Rev. 3:20? "Behold I stand at the

door and knock; if any man hear my VOICE." It is His voice that knocks! The fact that the word she uses is "knocketh", indicates that in her dream he knocked many times. It only takes one knock if the door is immediately opened. Did you ever hear a voice knock? He knocks but she is apathetic. Her apathy is underscored here in a couple of ways.

THE TIME WAS WRONG

"My head is filled with dew, and my locks with the drops of the night."

The wording suggests that Solomon arrived home in the early hours of the morning when the dew was falling. It other words it was VERY LATE! Perhaps some political strategy meeting had kept him at the palace, or some economic problem troubling the kingdom needed attention. Whatever the reason, Solomon was late getting home. He was wrong!

Husbands, see to it you get home early. Unlike Solomon, you can phone and explain the reason for being late. Never let suspicion put down roots in the mind of your wife. Jealousies can easily develop.

"Open to me..."

When Solomon arrived home he found she had locked the door on him! It sounds very much like the Church of Laodicea (Rev. 3:20). Of course they too had become LUKEWARM in love (Rev. 3:16). That lukewarm indifference closed the door on the One who loved them and sought entrance. Oh, the hardness of our hearts that would make Him knock so long! We are not too touched by His feelings, though He is by ours.

THE THOUGHT WAS WRONG

5:3 "I have taken off my housecoat; how shall I put it on?"

The second illustration of apathy is seen in her thinking. It was selfish reasoning. Her answer to his "open to me", was, "I don't feel like it!" She dreams her husband comes to her with

71

love on his mind and she is rather put out. "Can't you see I am in bed already? I was sound asleep! Do you expect me to get up again? My hair is in curlers and I don't want it messed up!" What a contrast to her feelings and attitude before their marriage (3:1-4)!

"I have washed my feet; how shall I defile them?"

The Shulamite does not want to get out of bed, put on her robe, walk across the cold floor, and open the door for him. After all she had bathed and gotten in bed, and now the pillow was shaped just right and at the desired temperature. Let it wait!

She had forgotten that the whole purpose of her beauty preparations had been for Solomon's sake, and that apart from him there was no reason to prepare.

How full of excuses we are when trying to justify ourselves, and how trivial they are. It makes us blush to review them! How full of "I" we are! Four I's appear in this short verse. Self occupation is evident here, and that is generally the cause of our indifference.

In the midst of being a dutiful and busy wife she had forgotten why and for whom she was living and doing. In thinking about herself she forgot her husband. And the excuse she gave was not really much of an excuse. Her reasons were trivial. Yet how many withhold love from their spouse over such stupid things. Like what does washing feet have to do with making love?

5:4 - My beloved put in his hand by the hole of the door ...and my heart yearned for him

She dreams that Solomon is not trying to unlock the door; that he would not force himself upon her. He rather puts in his hand to leave a token of love for her. She senses in her dreams that she should rise and let him in. BUT SHE RESPONDS TOO LATE!

5:5 - "I rose up to my beloved and my hands dropped with myrrh..."

She was heartbroken when finally she responded and

found he was gone!

5:6 - "I opened to my beloved, BUT he had withdrawn himself AND WAS GONE!"

Contrary to her expectations Solomon did not become angry. He simply left her a "love note" and then withdrew. It was customary to leave messages in the opening of the door if no answer was forthcoming. And the custom of lovers was to leave sweet smelling perfume, or ointment, on the handles of the door. In that way they said, "I missed you, and love you very much."

Instead of leaving evidence of love, most husbands, when rebuffed sexually, tend to become surly, withdraw into a shell of silence, or react with cutting words. But Solomon demonstrates true love. He responds properly by exhibiting kindness toward his wife, and patience in the Lord to work matters out.

Solomon was a wise man indeed, and realized anger would only bolster the indifferent attitude. Patient love made a difference and helped to awaken love in her. Notice now her reactions toward his actions.

5:6b - My soul failed...I called...no answer."

When Solomon did not beat on the door and carry on, but graciously withdrew, she immediately began to feel guilty! At that point another problem was created.

Have you ever noticed that one problem leads to another? Have you ever realized how disharmony in a relationship affects other aspects of life as well? When one gets "out of sorts" things begin to snowball quickly.

What is God teaching us here? The message is clear! God is teaching that it is never right to withhold sex from your spouse! You not only hurt your spouse but yourself as well.

The New Testament builds on this and clarifies the matter. Paul sets forth the principle that husband and wife are to render due benevolence to each other. Look again at First Corinthians, Chapter Seven.

I Cor. 7:3 - Notice that both husband and wife have equal

responsibility. And Paul has the sexual aspect in mind. The husband is to render the wife DUE benevolence. She is due it! The husband is not only to support the wife, but must satisfy her in this intimate area. "And likewise the wife unto the husband!" That means he also has due sexual benevolence coming. She is not rendering love as a slave, but as a partner. They owe it to each other!

I Cor. 7:4 - NEITHER ONE HAS A RIGHT TO WITH-HOLD THEIR BODY FROM THE OTHER! The wife has as much right and power over her husband's body, as does he of her. Doubtless there are some who are unreasonable in their demands.

I Cor. 7:5 - "Defraud ye not one another." That means to never withhold sex from the other. To abstain is not a sign of spirituality; it is a sign of selfishness! God looks on sexual defrauding as premeditated theft. To defraud is to withhold by deception that which rightfully belongs to another!

"Except it be by consent..." Abstinence in sex between a husband and wife is only acceptable when they both understand the reason why, and agree. They talk it over!

"For a time...and come together again, THAT SATAN TEMPT YOU NOT FOR YOUR INCONTINENCE!" In other words, never wait too long to resume sexual relations because Satan knows your needs and weaknesses, and will greatly tempt you because of vulnerability in this area. Incontinence is "lack of control". Neither husband or wife may be able to handle a prolonged period apart. Either party places themselves in great danger by withdrawing from the other sexually. One may feel no personal need for sex at a given time, but love should make them willing to satisfy their spouse. Therein may lie the secret of many happily married couples.

An elderly lady in one of my pastorates was like a mother to me, and like a grandmother to our family. She was a godly lady, and to call on her was always a delight. She lived with an infectious sense of humor and a cheerful outlook. She was forever extolling her husband, though he had been dead for many years. One day I asked her how it was that she and her husband got along so well and enjoyed life so much together. And this godly lady almost knocked me off my chair with her answer. A little quirk of a smile began working at the corner of her mouth, and she demurely said, "Pastor, I made sure I was always ready when he was!" They never defrauded one another!

"Except it be with consent for a time, that ye may give yourselves to fasting and prayer." Abstinence is in no way spiritual, but is often necessary to allow prolonged time to be given spiritual matters. Sexual abstinence without consent of your spouse is self-serving, and satan- serving.

Let no one assume that sex is everything, for it surely is not. But let everyone understand its importance and right use in the sight of God.

5:7-8 - "The watchmen found me .. smote me...wounded me ...took away my veil.

In the progression of the Shulamite's dream she went out into the city to find the one she loved, and suffered great physical abuse for it. She was treated like a woman of the streets!! What a dream! Imagine her trauma! A Queen being thought of as a prostitute! She was emotionally slain.

But her dream taught her several valuable things --

First, THAT A LAPSE OF LOVE ALWAYS RESULTS IN SUFFERING. The bride had not only hurt herself, but her husband. She also suffered the reproach of the world. We are always left wounded when we spurn our Lord.

Secondly, THAT THIS WORLD IS NO HELP TO US IN TRUE LOVE. This world is no friend to grace, to home, or to love. The world will somehow find us out, smite us, and make sport of our testimonial veil.

Thirdly, THAT KNOWING HIS LOVE WAS ALL THAT REALLY MATTERED. Furthermore the Shulamite determined that if she ever got things straightened out between her and Solomon, regardless of how she felt, she would always respond to his desires.

"Tell him I am sick of love!"

Solomon must know how sorry she is for refusing him. The indication is that from now on it will not be a matter of duty or obligation that will motivate her, but love for him! Would not any husband love his wife for feeling that way?

Mrs. Solomon is sick about what happened. There is now understanding that when one truly loves they do not feel used! She also realizes that life would not be worth living without him; that she could not make it without him.

Every marriage will have problems, but a successful marriage will work through the problems. The first problem set forth in this Song is the problem of Indifference on the part of the wife. This in turn raised a potential problem on the part of the husband. His pride might be wounded. His masculinity could be offended. He might go off to pout awhile and reveal childishness. But none of these things happen, and the two lovers reveal a move toward reconciliation.

The context presents two necessary steps in reconciliation. Both steps are introduced by questions. "WHAT is thy beloved more than another beloved" (5:9) and, "WHITHER is thy beloved gone" (6:1)? How do you answer the WHAT and the WHITHER questions?

The two questions put to her make the Shulamite realize how much she had concentrated on the negative rather than the positive side of her husband.

THE BIG QUESTION

5:9 "WHAT is thy beloved more than another beloved?"

Answer this, child of God, WHAT is there in Jesus Christ that makes Him more to you than any other? The world laughs, for they see nothing about Him that they desire. How do you answer?

The watchmen of the city were implying, "What makes him so special?" That is a good question for every wife. What is there about your husband that makes him better for you than someone else? Too many have decided there is nothing to be desired in their husband, and that another would be far better.

As the Shulamite ponders that question in her dream she enters into a reflective mood.

"O thou fairest among women..."!

She is now thinking of her own beauty. Twice she has been asked in this verse, "What is thy beloved more than another?" And in between they remind her that she is the fairest among women. They mean, "If you are so beautiful, why do you need our help in finding your husband?" That is like saying, "If you are so smart why aren't you rich?" Would not Solomon return home if she really were the best? If she were so pretty how come she did not have good sense? If she had used her head this would not have happened. The most beautiful woman in the world can become quite unappealing if she is self-centered.

"Tell him, that I am sick of love." (5:8b)

They had asked her WHAT made him better than others, and she concluded that it made no difference what others thought. Solomon was the only one for her, and she loved him! She wanted to find him and tell him she was sorry.

It has been said that "Beauty is in the eye of the beholder". There sure is a lot of truth in that when it comes to marriage. Some of the oddest looking opposites fall in love and marry. But regardless of how they are or look, if they believe their spouse is the only one for them, that is all that matters.

We are now ready for her answer to the question. As she dreams on we are given her description of WHAT Solomon is to her.

5:10 - "My beloved is white and ruddy, the chiefest among ten thousand."

The thrust of the thought here is, "He is the best looking man around!" He stands out among all others. The word "white" is rendered RADIANT! In our day she would probably have said, "To me he is STUNNING!"

The word "ruddy" holds the idea of MANLY! To her Solomon was one in ten thousand, a real man. He was the standard bearer among the multitudes.

5:11 - "His head is as the most fine gold..."

To the Shulamite, Solomon was a GOD MAN! We would say that he was like Christ. Remember that he had spoken of her godliness. Now she speaks of his. Solomon was made of the finest material. He was Number One in her heart.

Wives, how do you really feel about your husband? Does he have first place in your heart in comparison to all others? Or do you feel that he is a crud that does nothing right? Does he sense you feel that way? There was a man who had a wife that could never speak well of him. He left her and took up with a far less attractive woman, one far less talented. He justified it by saying, "She thinks I'm special!"

"His hair is bushy (wavy), and black as a raven."

Solomon was what you might call, "Tall, dark and handsome".

5:12 - "His eyes are as the eyes of doves..."

She thinks now of his LOYALTY to her, as well as his LOVE. The two go together. Dove's eyes represent both love and loyalty. No quality in a husband is so crucial to his wife's response as that of loyalty to her! Remember how your loyalty vows went? "Until death do us part; I pledge thee my troth (love)." Oh men, never lose the dove's look in your eyes! Disloyalty will kill as sure as dynamite.

5:13 - "His cheeks are as a bed of spices..."

Solomon always smelled good! There was much in him to enjoy. How like our Lord. "Unto you therefore which believe HE IS PRECIOUS." (1 Pet. 2:7).

"His lips like lilies..."

He was also a good kisser! He not only smelled good, he tasted good. She said his lips were as lilies, "dripping liquid myrrh"!

Who does not like kissing? How wonderful the kiss of love. But the kissing of today has lost its beauty and meaning. What is visualized before us in an exercise in nonsense. It is not kissing, it is chewing! Imagine two people going at each other like they were both trying to gnaw on an ear of sweet corn at the same time!

Never withhold kisses from your spouse. When couples do not show such affection to each other it makes one apprehensive about what may be going on in their lives and home! Be quick to kiss. And be quick to "Kiss the Son" (Psalm 2:12)

5:14 - "His hands are as gold rings set with beryl."

Oh those beautiful hands that minister to me! What language in a touch! Solomon was ever ready to place a gentle hand on her shoulder to comfort, or on her elbow to guide. And the rings of his hands spoke of his Godlike unchanging love for her.

What is there about a man's hands? Most women revere the hands of their husband. Those hands may be rough as a cob, calloused by hard work, big as scoop shovels, but they speak of strength and character. The roughest hands may be most gentle; and it is the sensitivity shown by those hands that speak so strongly. Men, are our hands mannerly and ministering?

"His belly (body) is as bright ivory overlaid with sapphire."

Solomon's body is revered by his wife for it houses the person she loves. How could it be less than beautiful to her? Plus, the body was probably enhanced by rippling muscles!

5:15 - "His legs are as pillars of marble..."

The legs of Solomon were strong and stately; not like match sticks! He would not be shaken when the winds of adversity blew.

His legs were as pillars of marble set upon bases of fine gold. In this the king was like our Lord. How different from Daniel's image which is a picture of man's dominion. It began well as God had planned a head of gold, but ended in toes of clay, typifying man's miserable failure. When the Greater than Solomon comes to reign, there will be no failure in His kingdom. Might and majesty alone belong to Him.

"His countenance is as Lebanon, excellent as the cedars."
Solomon was very impressive to look upon. He stood tall and
straight like the cedars of Lebanon. There was a natural dignity
to him.

5:16 - "His mouth is most sweet... !"

The mouth refers to his speech, not to the lips (as in verse
13). Oh the graciousness of his speech! It is said of our Lord, in
Luke 4:22, that they "wondered at the GRACIOUS WORDS
which proceeded out of His mouth." "No man ever spake as
this man" (John 7:46). This verse gives us four wonderful
things about Solomon.

HIS COMMUNICATION

"His mouth is most sweet"! The words "most sweet" mean
DOUBLY SWEET! Solomon spoke of his wife with utmost
kindness and graciousness. What wife would not appreciate
that? A wife's response to her husband is greatly affected by
the way he talks to her.

HIS CHARACTER

"He is altogether lovely"! The truth is that everything the
Shulamite saw about Solomon was wonderful. Again the word
"lovely" is plural. That is why it is translated "Altogether"! Solomon is more than just lovely; he is lovely in every way. He is
the loveliest!

HIS COMPLETENESS

"Altogether lovely"! In just two words the spouse seals her
summary of love. She had just tendered a tenfold discourse as
to why she thought her Beloved more than any other, and after
surveying him from head to foot, the quintessence of her witness was, "He is Altogether lovely"!

When attempting to contemplate the depth of our Lord's loveliness we find it is so great that we become aware of the shortness of our plumbline. The ocean of His loveliness is so vast that our rafts seem driven far out of sight of land, and we fear to spread the sail. His loveliness is overwhelming and inebriating. It acts on the heart like a live coal from off the altar. We may pass into a state of rapture, find our hearts burning within us, become dumb with pure ecstasy, mount up with wings as eagles, our soul becoming like the chariots of Amminadib; for what we cannot express we experience.

Let our eyes be cleansed until they become as the eyes of doves by the rivers of waters. He is All in All. He is altogether lovely!

HIS COMPANIONSHIP

"This is my beloved...my friend"! As the Shulamite dreams of what Solomon is to her more than another, she realizes he is her friend! He is more than a Lover and Husband, he is a Friend! In the long run it is that friendship that makes the walk through life a pleasant one. She wants to believe he is her BEST friend! She wants to know she can share anything and everything with him without being judged or attacked or ridiculed for it. She wants his counsel and encouragement. She wants to know what he thinks about what she says, or feels, or does. His FRIENDSHIP thus summarized her thoughts as to WHY her husband was more special to her than any other person.

We feel the same way about our lovely Lord, and find our heart singing, "There's no other such a Friend and Brother...."

Chapter Nine

THE RENEWAL OF ROMANCE

In answer to the first question the Bride described in great detail why Solomon was so special to her. That passage is important for all to understand. Wives need praise and encouragement from husbands, and husbands need praise and encouragement from their wives. It is a reciprocal requirement. The husband needs to know how much he is loved by his wife and why he is special to her; and the wife needs to know and hear the same from her husband. Has your spouse ever heard you say, "I love you. You are more to me than all the world. I could not live without you"? With what joy Solomon must have written the sweet words voiced by his wife!

Without argument marriage can become quite tense at times; and often for the dumbest reasons. The most trivial matter may become a giant barrier. Most will confess to sheer stupidity at times, and to the making of mountains out of molehills. But it happens! Many marriages might be saved were it not for little molehills becoming large mountains.

If marital difficulties are going to be solved, there must be constant remembrance of the commitment promised each other. That commitment was "for better or worse; for richer or poorer; in sickness and in health"! Most have discovered that things do not get much better, and seldom richer, and health has a way of going haywire on us. But loving commitment will stand by the one loved.

The ability of a couple to succeed in marriage is equal to how they hold to that commitment Everything may hinge on their ability to forgive and accept forgiveness. A broken relationship may result. How loving are you in forgiving? How loving are you after you have been forgiven? Can you be gracious in forgiving, and in receiving forgiveness?

The sixth chapter gives and answers the second question "Whither is thy beloved gone?" It also provides an insight into Solomon's gracious attitude in forgiving, and the Bride's response. Where Solomon went reveals so much about him and his grace. And what we do after a problem in our marriage relationship will tell so much about us.

THE BIGGER QUESTION

6:1 -"Whither is thy beloved one?"

By way of rebuke to the Shulamite, the daughters of Jerusalem say, "If your beloved is so special and so precious to you, why have you allowed him to slip out of your life?" By the same token, child of God, why do we repeatedly fall into the same snare of indifference that causes our Lord to withdraw fellowship from us?

"Where is he...that we may seek him with thee?"

After hearing the Shulamite's grand description of Solomon, they want to find him too! Is that not a lesson on why we ought always to EXTOL our Lord. Others will want to see for themselves the One who is Altogether lovely!

6:2 - "My beloved is gone down into his garden...to feed.. and to gather.

This is another way to say, "He's got work to do. And that is part of marital understanding. Solomon's commitment to her did not mean he could forsake his responsibilities as King. Affairs of state had to be attended to, and they had called him away the night she had spurned his advances. True, he came home late, but did she not understand it might be this way when they married? It was his responsibility to "FEED THE FLOCK"; to take care of his people.

By the way, this also pictures Solomon's SPIRITUAL LEADERSHIP as husband. He did not waver because of her indifference to him. He did right in the sight of God. She knew he was this kind of man. Therefore, despite what happened, she knew exactly where he had gone. He had gone to the garden! Would it not be wonderful if wives could say, following a dispute, I know where my husband is...he is in God's Word (garden) gathering goodies! Our set-to has not changed him spiritually! He is my stay!

6:3 -"I am my beloved's and my beloved is mine."

Did you notice the order is reversed from what she said in 2:16? Why the change? Now she says "I am my beloved's and my beloved is mine." Before she had said, "My beloved is mine, and I am his"! Does she here feel the need to reaffirm her COMMITMENT TO HIM? There are times when love calls for reaffirmation.

The Shulamite has been extolling the virtues of her husband, and it causes a renewal of her love. The cloud is suddenly lifted from her heart. She now understands that her commitment is to her husband regardless of what duties may take him away from her at times. Her statement is also a way of apologizing for the indifference that night when he came home late. How easy it is to become resentful when someone or something absorbs our spouse's time and energies. This is not uncommon in a pastor's home. Too frequently the preacher's wife feels her husband is shared with everyone but her. There are days, and nights, when that choice servant feels she has married a church and not a man. They find it difficult to have quality time alone. Too often the pastor is "off to feed the flock", and the wife is left to talk to the walls.

It is the commitment of marriage that provides firm boundaries within which problems can be worked out. It was so with the Shulamite. She knew she belonged to him, and that he belonged to her! She built on that!

The Shulamite knew where Solomon was all the time! Why then did she ask the daughters of Jerusalem where he was? She not only knew where her husband was, but that he would be waiting for her! It is here that Solomon furnishes a good example of one principle often necessary in resolving

85

marital conflict. SILENT PATIENCE! Patience will pave the way for reunion. It allows the dust to settle, and the heat to cool. It gave the Bride time to realize her offense. Then she was able to receive the forgiveness her husband was so ready to give.

6:4 - "Thou art beautiful, O my love..."

Note how gracious Solomon is. He surprises her with compliments instead of criticism! He was taking spiritual leadership.

Did you read between the lines here? Notice that she went to him! Notice also that he was WAITING FOR HER to come! Like the song goes, "He was there all the time"! And when she came he never mentioned her indifference, but praised her!

Her personal hurt and slight were overlooked, let alone a penance demanded for it. How like our adorable Lord who could fulfill I Corinthians 13. "Love thinketh no evil...beareth all things...believeth all things...endureth all things...Love never faileth"! And our Beloved never fails! His love never changeth! His love for us is not based on our behavior but on His own great Word and Work. I emanates from His own great heart of love and cannot be stopped! We may turn our backs but His love will shine upon our backs. We may grieve Him but we cannot stop Him from loving us. To Him we are His treasure, His delight, fair and comely with the beauty that He has conferred upon us.

To remain at a distance from our Lord, to not come to Him, is to insult His grace. To say it is because we are mourning our failures and weaknesses is to show that we are still occupied with self. Let us be done with the flesh. God does not expect anything of it, so why should we?

Too many feel that the distress they have brought upon themselves is nothing less than God's punishment; that He has turned against them. The silence is only the awareness of His patience as He waits for us to confess our wrong in not coming to Him for forgiveness. This portion stresses the fact that we mean more to Him than He could possibly ever mean to us. There is nothing dearer to God than His Bride!

Could it be that as this Bride went her way to meet Solomon she feared what he might say when they met? How unlike most men he was! He did not make her feel worse. He did not say, "Well you certainly are not the girl I thought I had married! " No, he spoke to her as lovingly as ever he had.

"Thou art beautiful...as terrible as an army of banners"!

The word "terrible" is equivalent to AWE-INSPIRING! He was conquered by her! She caused his heart to swell with love and pride. Three special descriptions are given of her: BEAUTIFUL...COMELY...TERRIBLE! All about her was awe-inspiring. He could do no less than surrender before such an army!

6:5 - "Turn away thine eyes from me..for they have overcome me"!

It appears the Shulamite came to Solomon with her head down. There was manifested an attitude of repentance. But when her husband spoke such glowing words of praise she lifted her head to look upon him. That loving worshipful look in her eyes was too much for Solomon. He said, "Turn away thine eyes, they OVERWHELM me"! Some say the word "overcome" should be rendered CONFUSE; as though she made him all a twitter by looking so lovingly at him.

Eyes can speak the love that is in the heart, when the mouth cannot. Eyes also are capable of sending messages carried by invisible darts.

6:6-7 - "Your hair...your teeth...thy temples...thy locks"!

Solomon is repeating things he said on his wedding night! Why the repetition? It was not because he was unable to find words wherewith to describe her, but rather because he wanted to assure her that HE FELT THE SAME WAY ABOUT HER NOW AS HE DID THEN! Nothing had changed with him!

So with us and our Lord. What can increase our love for Him like finding His love unchanged toward us in spite of our miserable failures and unfaithfulness!

How thoughtful and loving Solomon was as a husband.

He knew and understood his wife. Rather than retaliate, he restored! He set the pattern of love.

Checkpoint: I Peter 3:7 -- "You husbands dwell (live) with them (your wives) according to knowledge (in an understanding way)"! The verb DWELL WITH is consistently used in the Old Testament marriage setting to indicate the sexual aspect. And the phrase, "According to knowledge" (or understanding), implies acquiring that knowledge and insight through a process of personal investigation. Thus a free translation of this verse might read, "You husbands likewise, live in a sexual relationship with your wife in a way that is based upon insight gathered from personal investigation of HER NEEDS"!

Checkpoint: I Peter 3:9 - "Not returning evil for evil, or insult for insult, but contrariwise BLESSING INSTEAD"! Solomon, in wise understanding, rendered blessing instead!

Part of the sexual relationship with your spouse is, in an understanding way, NOT responding with insult when hurt, but responding with blessing; with love and appreciation for his or her strong qualities.

Checkpoint: I Peter 3: 10 - "For let him who means to LOVE LIFE, and see good days, refrain his tongue from evil..." To all who desire to improve the marital relationship, it is imperative that all responses to offenses be honoring to the Lord!! The quick tongue can be so devastating.

Perhaps you noticed that Solomon left out any mention of his wife's breasts or lips? He omits anything sensual or sexual in nature. He even asks that she turn her eyes from him, lest they arouse him. He did this that she might not think his interest was sexual. He guarded against any possible misconception on her part. He knew that when many men want to make up, the first thing most wives think is that sex is all they have in mind.

Solomon is praising her. "Sweetheart, you are the great-

est! Your love and friendship are what I want most of all."
When the love relationship is mended with stitches of love and
kindness, the sexual relationship will take care of itself.

6:8 - "There are sixty queens, and eighty concubines, and virgins without number"!

Solomon continues praising his wife. The verse is not implying that Solomon had all these women. It is not "I have", but
"There are". He is simply a loving husband making a lover's
comparison; Sixty, Eighty, and Without Number!

Solomon is vindicating her before others who may have
witnessed her defection. Peter was a sad failure, but after tender rebuke and secret restoration he was honored publicly. One
day the poor failing Church will be brought forth in glory and
beauty not her own and hailed as His heart's Beloved. Christ
said of that time, "I will make them come and worship before
thy feet and to know that I have loved thee." (Rev. 3:9).

There were many others, but Solomon says his wife alone
is unique. He was in no way regretting he had married her. She
was totally different. She was absolutely the greatest. In his
eyes she was without equal!

Solomon meant that if he had to do it all over again, he
still would choose her! Husbands and wives, at the risk of
sounding improper, if your spouse undertook to search for a
mate would they select you now that they know you? Would
you qualify as a Spouse, a Friend, a Lover? Would you be a
blessing, or fun to live with? If not then it would be in order to
consider making some needed changes.

6:9 - "My dove...she is the ONLY ONE...THE CHOICE ONE"!

Solomon did not pout and wander off into a dream world
where he could feel sorry for himself and wish he had married
another. Such an attitude would only have compounded the
problem. Quite the opposite. He creatively and compas-
sionately assured her of his forgiveness. She was the ONLY
ONE! She was still that special lady he married, and he was

thankful for her. There was no wounded pride on his part.

"The only one of her mother, she is the choice one of her..."

Solomon and her mother were in agreement on that! Here is a word of wisdom in passing; men it is a good thing to be in agreement with your mother-in-law about some things! Solomon was no dummy. Then too, Solomon probably knew that his mother-in-law was a better cook than his wife at this stage in their marriage!

"The daughters saw her, and BLESSED her; yea, the queens...PRAISED her"!

Not only her mother, but all others agreed that Solomon's wife was a choice one. Even the QUEENS! The word "blessed" means they congratulated her.

And if her praise came from the highest, surely it should come from her husband as well. They knew Solomon could have had any woman in the world, but he chose her. That made her special in their eyes.

Husbands, do as Solomon. Praise your wife by telling her the good things that others are saying about her. She needs to hear this from you too.

On the other hand, it is always good for husbands to let other women know how much their wife means to them. It helps eliminate attempts to undermine the marital bond. When a man criticizes his wife before other women, he is setting himself up for a possible fall. Some fool woman will think he needs her sympathy and care!

6:10 "Who is this that looketh forth as the morning, fair as the moon, clear as the sun, and terrible as an army..."

Solomon praises his wife in a four-fold descriptive:

    1.   BEAUTIFUL AS THE MORNING!
           She was as lovely as a new day! Her beauty grew on him!

    2.   FAIR AS THE MOON!
           She was a reflection of him. To him she was "clear" (PURE)!

    3.   BRIGHT AS THE SUN!

She outshines them all! She was radiant. "You light up my life!"

4. TERRIBLE AS AN ARMY!
    She was not terrible, as we think the word means, but Awe- Inspiring! Solomon surrendered to her like one would if facing an entire army. She was ir-resistible!

Let's face it, Solomon was in love with his wife! And if a man praised his wife like this she would surely think him to be special as well.

6:11 - "I went down into the garden of nuts..."

Some unwisely believe this has reference to the Church. There may be many "nuts" in the church, but this does not mean the Church. One pastor went home after a trying day and his wife asked him what was wrong. He replied, "I believe every kook in town comes to our church ' "

"To see whether the vine had budded, and the po-megranates had bloomed."

It appears that the Shulamite went to Solomon with some anxiety as to how he would respond over her refusal and in-difference. Was the TENDER VINE still like it was? Had those "little foxes" ruined it? She wanted reassurance that all was well; and everyone needs that at times.

Urgency gripped her heart, and she was running when she got to Solomon. Dignity was forgotten in her eagerness to be reconciled to her husband. She was coming like a racing chariot, tears unchecked were coursing down her cheeks, her hair trailing out in the wind. No wonder Solomon said, "Who is she?" (vs 10).

6:12 - "Before I was aware my soul had made me as the chariots of Ammi-nadib"

The beauty of it all is how the Shulamite discovered the DEPTH of Solomon's love and forgiveness. It translates, "Be-fore I realized it, my desire set me among the royal chariots of my people." In other words, so swift was her restoration that before she hardly realized it she was again riding in the royal chariot along side of Solomon! Everyone knew (in her dream) that they were together again! She was his Queen, honored above all others in his realm. He was not embarrassed to have everyone know that she was his bride and lover.

6:13 - "Return, return, O Shulamite..."

The word "return" is found four times here. In her dream the Shulamite hears her husband calling, "COME BACK, COME BACK"! The word "Shulamite" is the feminine form of the word "Solomon". One could say, Mrs. Solomon". In the dream then she heard him calling, "Come back, come back Mrs. Solomon, you are my wife!"

That title meant very much to her. How pleased she must have been to hear folks refer to her, or address her, as "Mrs. Solomon".

Mrs. Solomon! In her occupation with her beloved she had taken on his characteristics. She was becoming like him! Because Shulamite is the feminine form of the name Solomon we have a wonderful proof again of the inspiration and purpose of this passage. How beautifully this reference carries out the teaching of the Scriptures that we are the body and bride of the true Solomon, our Lord Jesus Christ. Bone of His bone, and flesh of His flesh.

"What will ye see in the Shulamite?"

In surprise she asks this question. She cannot imagine what they would care to look upon in her. The answer is seen in their response.

"As it were the company of two armies"!

This gives us the thought of two different companies meeting and becoming one! When Jacob met with the angels of God he recognized that there were two hosts with him, his own band and the band of God's angels. The effect of that meeting was blessing and power to Jacob, and his name was changed to Israel which means a prince of God. In the case of the Shulamite it was Queen with Solomon! She was one with him, and her name was now "Mrs. Solomon"!

While the Shulamite dreamed her conscience was working. She realized that she was Solomon's other part! That part of him was now missing! The daughters of Jerusalem are speaking but to her it is as though Solomon is calling. He is saying, "You belong to me. You are part of my life, and I am incomplete without you. Come back to me!"

TAKE A RELOOK!

The Shulamite went down into the garden because she knew her husband would be there. But she went with a fear! She went "to see if the vine FLOURISHED, and the pomegranates BUDDED! She wondered if it would be springtime for them again. Would love be renewed? Would there be a new season of love? Would it be like it once was?

Things seem to indicate that this occurred about a year after their wedding. That the cycle of the seasons had made a full turn, and it was coming into the spring season again, would bolster that thought.

What did the Shulamite find? SHE FOUND LOVE CAN KNOW SPRINGTIME AGAIN! That means you can get love back! It was her very move to her husband that did it. Before she knew it they were back together again, and she was his queen once more! She was forgiven, and loved as much as ever she was loved!

THE VERY NATURE AND RECEPTION OF FORGIVENESS MEANS SEEING YOURSELF AS THE OTHER PERSON SEES YOU! Thus at the moment you are forgiven your eyes are off yourself and on another. The Shulamite went to the garden in full hope of forgiveness and restoration, and was met with praise which turned her eyes from herself to HIM; and once to HIM then back to herself through his eyes of love and forgiveness.

Solomon still saw her as the woman he married. But, believe it or not, he no longer saw her "terrible as an army" (vv 4, 10), but "as it were the COMPANY OF TWO ARMIES!" The problem had worked out for blessing. She now was twice as

93

strong as before!

Hasten to resolve any marital problem, and you will be the stronger for it.

* * *

Christian marriage is intended of God as the primary witness to this world. It is a living, walking illustration of the relationship between Christ and the Church. Or to put it more broadly, it is to picture God's love for man and how man should respond to that love.

Is your marriage just an ordinary marriage? Or is it any better because you love Christ? Husbands have you asked God to help you love your wife as Christ loved the Church? Do you have any notion how Christ loves the Church? The truth is appealing that Christ loves you, but do you realize He loves your wife also? Now can He help you love her like He loves her? Can He share His love for your wife with you?

Is your love for your wife one that just uses her to satisfy fleshly desires, or is it a love that wants to see her flower and bloom and be the woman and wife God wants her to be? Knowing Christ should make the difference in the most precious earthly relationship a person can have. Knowing Christ should always enable us to keep the freshness in marriage, and make love grow better and better.

Chapter Ten

MAKING LOVE BETTER AND BETTER

There is no seeming end to joking about marriage. One man said he did not know what happiness was until he got married, but then it was too late! Another glibly stated that marriage is not a word, it is a sentence! Added to that is the one that marriage is an institution and love is blind; therefore marriage is an institution for the blind! From all appearances today many are deciding not to live their life in such an institution.

While much of the joking is just for laughs, it also may be the cover-up of serious problems. To look at many marriages today is to wonder if it is possible for a couple to really grow in love, and to experience a deepening and richer relationship as the years go by.

Certainly the all-wise God, the designer of love and marriage, did not intend for marital life to be a matter of misery. It was not intended to become a punishment or penalty for an initial few months of joy and happiness. Marriage is not to be a slow death, but an increasing delight.

Upon entering the seventh chapter of the Song of Solomon we find ourselves in the immediate presence of the king and his wife. We hear his highest praise of her. In chapter four Solomon mentioned seven qualities of his bride, but in this chapter he enlarges the list to TEN! The numbers seven and ten both speak of perfection and completion. But the fact that Solomon gives ten qualities seems to imply that she has grown on him. He understands her more fully.

In chapter four Solomon began the description of his

95

bride's beauty by mentioning the hair of her head. But in chapter seven he begins with her FEET! Let us apply our hearts and minds to a consideration of this ten-fold praise.

7:1 - "How beautiful are thy feet with shoes"!

This is Solomon's answer to the question, "What will ye see in the Shulamite?" (6:13). When Solomon looked at his bride in chapter four, and began to describe her hair, he was stressing her GLORY! But here, when he addresses the on-looking world, he points out her feet, or WALK! How appropriate that her feet be mentioned first.

There was a time when, like the Prodigal son, we walked in sin. But upon coming to the Father's house we were given SHOES for our feet The Shulamite has "come back" to Solomon, and so has shoes on her feet. Solomon is thinking of her right relationship to him. Her feet now are "beautiful", or GRACEFUL!

What do feet have to do with love? The Little Flower of my garden has pretty brown eyes, but her feet are another matter. But to God our feet are absolutely beautiful when they walk in His love! And how beautiful they are when we use them to go forth publishing glad tidings. Solomon saw his wife walking before him IN grace and WITH grace.

"O prince's daughter".

This does not indicate the Shulamite's pedigree, but her character. She was just a humble grape picker, but conducted herself with royal dignity! There was something regal about her.

We are just sinners saved by grace, but when we walk before our Lord in submissive obedience He sees our feet as beautiful (Rom. 10:15, Isa. 52:7). God loves to see our feet with His shoes; shod with the preparation of the Gospel of Peace (Eph. 6:15).

"The joints of thy thighs are like jewels, the work of a cunning man."

Solomon compares the curves of her thighs to "ornaments". God, the "cunning workman", had abundantly endowed her. Our daughter Kim came running home from kindergarten to quote us a common poem she had just learned; little Miss Muffett, sat on a tuffet, eating her curves away!"

"Thy navel is like a round goblet..."

"Thy belly is like a heap of wheat set about with lilies."

Solomon compares her abdomen to a rounded glass never lacking wine; and her stomach to a heap of wheat. WINE and WHEAT were the basic foods of every table. Thus he is saying that his wife was to him as a wonderful feast.

For some husbands to describe their wife's stomach as a "heap of wheat" could spell trouble.

"Thy two breasts are like two young roes that are twins."

The breasts speak of her affections, and Solomon accepted them as his. For all believers their AFFECTION (singular) belongs to the Bridegroom (Col. 3: 1-3) . That affection is not to be profligated, but entirely centered upon Him! All is wrapped up in ONE affection for Him.

"Thy neck is as a tower of ivory."

For some reason the female neck holds great affection for the male. They love to place their hands upon it. When the neck is fitly adorned with ornaments its beauty is greatly enhanced.

"Thine eyes like the fish pools of Heshbon, by the gate of Bath-rabbin."

Oh those lovely eyes! To Solomon his wife's eyes were clear and deep, like the pools of Heshbon. Through the gate of Bath-rabbin weary multitudes passed, then rested by the peaceful pools. Solomon is saying that in the midst of his busy life he could draw aside from its hurry and worry and find rest and peace with her.

"Thy nose is as the tower of Lebanon which looketh toward Damascus."

Much can be determined about one's character by the shape of the nose. One function of the nose is to smell. To the child of God this is of utmost importance. We need STRONG discernment (Heb. 5:14). No one with a flat or broken nose was allowed to minister to the Lord in the Old Testament. The Shulamite must have proven her spiritual discernment as strong, and Solomon was impressed with her nobility, character and spirituality.

7:5 - "Thine head upon thee is like Carmel."

Of all the physical characteristics of Solomon's wife, her head was to him the most beautiful. Like Carmel she stood out above all others. The head CROWNED her as Carmel crowned the land; strong and impressive. It proved a lovely crown for a lovely queen. No wonder Solomon would say, "Let me see thy face"!

An earthly king may never see in you the beauty desired to fit a queen, but rejoice in the fact that God has graciously stricken some men with love-blindness. If your husband insists on saying you are the most beautiful person he has ever seen, do not argue with him...let it be!

"The hair of thine head like purple."

Again Solomon stresses the fact that she is queenly to him. Since purple was the color of royalty, he sees her hair as a crown of glory.

"The king is held in the galleries."

Imagine that! A mighty king HELD captive by hair! There is nothing more alluring, seductive, or captivating to a man, than a woman's hair. How pleasant to run the fingers through it, enjoy the fragrance of it, and lay the face next to it.

Wives, keep your hair looking lovely if at all possible. It is your GLORY (I Cor. 11:15). Never remove that crown! Paul says it is a shame for a woman to cut her hair so short she looks like a man! God intended sexual distinctions be maintained between male and female because this affects sexual attraction and sexual roles and relationships.

A woman's hair is a mark of femininity. Her husband may be held captive by it! The fact that the Shulamite's hair is mentioned last seems to suggest it is the culmination of her beauty. Whereas on the wedding night Solomon praised her in a seven-fold way, he now praises her in a ten-fold way. HE

WAS TELLING HER SHE WAS GETTING BETTER AND BET-
TER! She was growing in perfection!

Husbands, we ought to be able to praise our wives by re-
minding them that they mean more to us all the time; that we
love them more now than when we married. Love should be a
continuum; always deepening and strengthening.

The ten-fold descriptive sequence of praise included:

1. Her feet (in shoes). She was dainty!
2. Her thighs (curvacious).
3. Her abdomen (like a costly, shaped bowl).
4. Her stomach (like a heap of fine wheat).
5. Her breasts (as twin fawns).
6. Her neck (like ivory).
7. Her eyes (as peaceful pools).
8. Her nose (as the stately tower of Lebanon).
9. Her head (like a crown of Carmel).
10. Her hair (like royal tresses).

7:6 - "How fair and how pleasant art thou O love, for de-
lights."

As though the ten-fold praise was not sufficient, Solomon
continues to heap on more compliments. Listen, husbands, one
of the best ways to prepare your wife for lovemaking is to give
her constant words of praise. Solomon is our role model in this
matter.

"Delights"!

The word "delights" is better translated CHARMS! Solomon describes the enjoyment he saw and experienced in her.
She must have been a wonderful person to be around.

7:6 - "How pleasant ..for delights."

In ways understandable to his wife, Solomon begins to describe how delightful and pleasant she was to him.

7:7 - "Thy stature is like to a palm tree".

Here again we get the idea of both her uprightness and inner life. It is said that the palm tree, even though bent down,
will spring to its upright position when released. The Arabs
have a saying about the palm tree, that it stands with its feet in

salt water and its head in the sun. They often cannot drink the brackish water found in the oasis where the palm tree grows, so tap the tree and drink the sweet palm wine. Somehow, by the magic of its inner life, the palm tree can change the elements found in the unkindly soil around it and make them minister to its growth and strength and fruit bearing. The Shulamite was like the palm tree.

7:8 - "The smell of thy nose is like apples".

It seems to mean that her breath was like the sweet smell of apples. She did not prepare for lovemaking by partaking of leeks, onions and garlic.

7:9 - "The roof of thy mouth is like the best wine..."

There is a break in this ninth verse. Solomon begins by saying, "The roof of thy mouth is like the best wine", and his wife places her finger on his lips to halt him, and inject the words, "That goeth down smoothly for my beloved." She wishes to assure him that all she is or has is for him alone.

"Causing the lips of those that are asleep to speak."

The King's love has unlocked her lips, and so it will with us if we allow it. The best wine of heaven is ours for the taking and will assuredly unlock our silent lips and cause praise to flow forth. Oh the joy of His wine!

7:10 - "I am my beloved's, and his desire is toward me".

The Shulamite thrills at the fact that her husband desires her. To her love meant contentment because of COMMITMENT. "I am my beloved's..." It is that complete commitment to each other in marriage that produces the highest level of contentment. It also creates the proper marital environment in which God intended sexual pleasure to be enjoyed.

COMPLETE COMMITMENT

When the garden of Love and Marriage is constantly cultivated and cared for, the result is that it becomes better and better, more beautiful and more fruitful. The welfare of love's tender plants involves the complete commitment of each other.

As the commitment grows, so does the garden.

Solomon presents three stages of growth in commitment seen in the Shulamite. It will do us well to review those stages. The commitment clause stated in verse ten is slightly altered from the other two times it was given. Note the growth pattern:

1. "My beloved is mine, and I am his" (2:16)
   Here she is thinking of what she has in Solomon!
2. "I am my beloved's, and my beloved is mine" (6:3).
   Now she is thinking of what Solomon has in her!
3. "I am my beloved's, and his desire is toward me (7:10).
   The ultimate concern is, what does he want from her!

During the courtship days a commitment was needed for personal SANCTITY, the keeping of themselves for each other. Once married there was a commitment needed for SUBMISSION; that personal differences and problems be rightly solved. As marriage progressed, a commitment was necessary for STABILITY to halt any wavering or withdrawing of love; and so assure the unselfish, unstinting living to please the other.

When the Shulamite first mentioned that Solomon was hers, she was placing her possession of him primary. The second time she mentions that Solomon was hers, she reverses the order and makes his possession of her primary. The third time she mentions that Solomon was hers, she places his possession of her not only primary, but strengthens it by adding that his desire is toward her. IN OTHER WORDS SHE HAD BECOME FOCUSED ON HIM! She now omits her possession of him, and emphasizes his possession of her! SHE HAS LOST HERSELF IN HIM AND THUS FOUND HERSELF! Prayerfully ponder that as you read Matthew 10:39!

"His desire is toward (for) me".

The word "desire" is very carefully chosen. It is used only two other times in Scripture. The first time is Genesis 3:16 where the curse of mankind would be the woman's excessive, perhaps unreturned, desire toward her husband. Yet, in the

Song of Solomon we find that the husband's desire is toward his wife! It is almost as though the Scripture was saying, that in a truly ideal marriage, part of the curse on mankind is reversed!

No child of God should rest content that he is saved and now belongs to the Lord. Salvation, security, and service are all important, but there is something of greater importance. Like the Shulamite, it was not enough to just belong to Solomon and to assert her claim on him. We must keep in mind and give absolute priority to our Lord's claim on US! That which holds greater importance is to have our heart so occupied with our Lord that we lose sight of everything else and delight our souls fully in His love.

CONSTANT CREATIVITY

7:11 - "Come, my beloved, let us go forth into the field, let us lodge in the village."

The Shulamite is not simply talking, she is doing something. She is attending to her garden. She is creating a love environment for the two of them. This is her labor of love. She recognizes the need for privacy and change. Therefore she plans some special places where they can go, and some special things they can do, TOGETHER! She wanted no more separation!

The Shulamite is responding to her husband's desire "FOR" her; thus her unveiling of a creative program to make their marriage relationship better.

7:12 - "Let us...let us..."

Again we find those words, "let us". Four times they occur in these two verses. Solomon's wife has determined that they must do things together. She is excited about her plans. Thankfully Solomon did not pour cold water on them.

"There will I give thee my loves".

Her special plans provide for some intimate moments! She is indicating to Solomon that some surprises are in store for him.

7:13 - "The mandrakes give a smell".

The Arabs called the mandrakes "the servant of love". They believed the exotic fragrance of the mandrakes was conducive to love. The pleasing perfume placed one in the mood for love. The Shulamite would use common inexpensive means to put newness and freshness into her love responses. That proves enjoyable to any husband.

"At our gates are all manner of pleasant fruits, new and old".

Variety is said to be the spice of life. Could the routine of sameness be what staggers so many couples? After years of marriage the common complaint is that it is always the same old thing; nothing ever new! It takes constant creativity on the part of both to produce an atmosphere of freshness in marriage.

The important thing to keep in mind is the need of the spouses for YOUR creativity. One look at them may convince you their case is hopeless. Never believe it! No matter how dull or boring your spouse may appear to be, your love responses are desired and needed. Never give up because they have no ideas or plans. That may be true. If so, you be the creative one. There is no excuse for things to be always "OLD". Be committed enough to initiate and innovate change. Complete commitment and constant creativity will guarantee love and marriage growing better and better.

"Things both new and old."

The Shulamite remembers with thanksgiving the first things, when she was a poor maiden of the vineyards, blackened by the hot winds and sun. Then she recalls how her beloved Solomon came into her life filling it with joy and gladness, lavishing upon her his great love and wealth, showing her such care and solicitude as to win her heart. He had brought her into his house of banqueting and seated her at the royal table, unfurling over her his banner of love that all might see that she had found favor in his sight. Wonderful memories of love!

And then the NEWER things, such as his wonderful grace in restoring her to favor when her careless heart had caused her to stray from him, to sleep when he needed her, and to resist his advances of love. Wonderful grace had melted her heart and made it cleave to him. She has fruits both new and old and they are jealously kept for him. No sharing of them with others. No giving of them to the world as we sometimes do.

Love so amazing, so divine, demands my life, my soul, my all. Success in marriage, as well as success in christian living, calls for total commitment.

Chapter Eleven

THE GREATEST OF THESE IS LOVE

When Solomon was choosing his Bride he was also choosing a lifelong companion. More than a wife, she would also be to him a Friend (5:16), a spiritual Sister (8:1), a Student (8:2), and Lover (8:14).

Likewise in Solomon, the Shulamite received a Lover (5:16), a Friend (5:16), a Brother (8:1), a Teacher (8:2), and a Companion (8:5); all comprised in one husband! All they needed they found answered in the other. Together they experienced completeness.

In becoming united with Christ we too obtain much more than just a Bridegroom. In Him we are complete, and never want. In Him all needs are supplied. He is:

1. Our Shepherd who leads us (Psalm 23).
2. Our Friend who gives His life for us (Jh. 15:13).
3. Our Confidant who shares with us (Jh. 13:18).
4. Our Servant who cleanses us (Jh. 13:1-10, I Jh. 1:9).
5. Our Teacher who instructs us (Jh. 16:13).
6. Our Companion who never leaves us (Matt. 28:30, Heb. 13:5).
7. Our Lover, and Husband (Eph. 5:25).
8. Our Lord, yet our Brother (Rom. 8:29).

Blest be these ties that bind us, and these bonds of relationship become stronger as all those lovely aspects are realized and fulfilled.

8:1 - "O that thou wert as my brother... I would kiss thee..."

The Shulamite is playfully assuming the role of an older

sister to a younger brother. She would smother "her baby" with kisses like a mother who had just found her little one wandering "without" (outside the house).

8:2 - "I would lead thee..."

She would lead him back to safety. Then she adds, "and thou would instruct (teach) me"! The Shulamite is laughing as she coyly suggests having authority over him, but quickly gives way to admission of his leadership over her ——

"I would cause thee to drink of spiced wine..."

This is the ancient version of an apple for the teacher!

8:3 - "His left hand...his right hand..."

Note that in these three brief verses she had indicated she knew her husband as a Brother (vs 1), Teacher (vs 2), and Lover (vs 3). And what a lover!

Like God's hands, Solomon's hands would hold her close. Those arms are everlasting arms. They never cease to embrace and hold us. The Bride is confessing another outgrowth of love in her realization of his protecting providence.

The right hand of God seems to absorb most of our thinking in Scripture, but never forget the loving ministry of His LEFT hand! God's right hand is Power for us; His left hand is Pleasure for us. Those lovely hands never fail us.

8:4 - "I charge you...stir not up, nor awake my love, until he pleases".

Twice before the Shulamite had made this charge as a warning against premarital or extramarital sex (2:7 and 3:5). Now she serves final notice on this world that she belongs wholly to Solomon. Each warning, including this one, emphasizes the POWER of sexual desire. Even after marriage sex must be controlled; or it will create great problems within ourself, as well as a long lasting hurt in the spouse.

Marriage is not a one-sided commitment. The Shulamite is taking her husband into consideration as well as herself. Love thinketh of the other! The truth is most husbands and wives do not really take time to love. Even their most intimate times are hurried and forced. Such impatience and thoughtlessness can become terrible enemies to marriage. She knew Solomon would do right.

WHAT IS LOVE?

Someone has said that love is the strange tickling sensation in the pit of your stomach. Perhaps many have mistaken such a feeling to be evidence of real love. However our Lord clarified love by placing it in the light of giving, not feeling (Jh. 3:16). Paul characterized love in these words, "Christ loved the Church and gave Himself for it" (Eph. 5:25). And with that verse Paul also made it known that is the way husbands are to love their wives. They are to emulate the love of Christ for His Bride, the Church.

The thirteenth chapter of First Corinthians seems to define love for us. Love is seen as Indispensable, Incomparable, and Indestructible. The qualities of love are set forth, and the summation is that love never fails! It never behaves itself unseemly, seeketh not her own, suffereth long, and is kind. It abides! It surpasseth! The greatest thing of all is love!

One day a troubled woman came to my study where she poured out her heart over the fact that love had failed. She felt her marriage was on the rocks, that the love she had had for her husband was dead. I assured her that it was possible to learn to love again. At the conclusion of our talk I wrote down for her several choice verses of Scripture, including the great love chapter of First Corinthians, and asked her to read them everyday. She was to read them aloud three times a day, as regularly as though she were taking prescription medicine. Would you believe that in about three weeks her husband came to me, knowing nothing at all of our conversation, and with amazement told of the wonderful change that had taken place in his wife. She had gotten her mind off herself and had become concerned about giving herself lovingly to her husband.

In these next few verses Solomon sets before us four great characteristics of love. Operating within the marital bounds they are seen as Personal, Possessive, Powerful, and Priceless.

LOVE IS AN INTIMATE COMMITMENT

8:5 - "Who is this that cometh up from the wilderness, leaning upon her beloved?"

Using binoculars one can see the couple off in the distance, strolling together. Her head is gently laying on his shoulder, and his arm is tight about her.

Solomon says she was "leaning". Some have rendered it as "cleaving" to him. There can be no leaning on another unless there is complete trust in them. She had been weaned away from all earthly supports, and is now resting upon Solomon as her all in all.

"Cometh UP"!

Again, she was leaning upon the Beloved because her route was an ascending one. The Bride's way is up. She is on the upward way. The married life ought always to be upward, always getting better and better. Our Lord brought us UP out of the wilderness, and now we lean upon HIM and delight in His ability to take care of us.

"I awoke thee under the apple tree, there...there..."

We must never forget that all we are and have we owe to our Beloved. Let us not forget where we have been, and what we were, and what love has done for us. It will cause us to lean lovingly and intimately upon our Lord.

8:6 - "Set me as a SEAL upon thine heart...as a SEAL upon thine arm."

What a grand request love makes! Possession of another's seal means free access to all that they possess. The heart is the source of AFFECTION, and the arm is the source of STRENGTH. One is Inward, the other Outward. She lays claim to possessing both Solomon's heart and strength. She wants all to know she is the closest thing to Solomon's heart; And that is her right!

God sealed us with the Holy Spirit because of our great

value to Him. That seal speaks of a transaction that is settled. His love for us makes it unmistakably clear that we mean more to Him than anything else in this world! It means we are His possession forever! The Shulamite bride wanted the private and personal seal of love on both his heart and arm. Love demands such an intimate commitment.

"Set ME as a seal..."

Set me as a seal upon thine HEART. Make me to know and never forget that I am Thine, the object of Thy love. Set me as a seal upon thine ARM. Help me always to remember that I have no strength apart from Thee. Without Thee I am nothing.

LOVE IS AN INTENSE COMMITMENT

8:6 - "Love is strong as death"!

Love is strong as death. This is why the bride implores the bridegroom to set her as a seal upon his heart, as a seal upon his arm. She has learned to know and trust his love for her. Oh the strength of love! One can no more reverse death than one can reverse true love. Death is so strong that only God can break it. God can break death, but God will not break love.

"Jealousy is cruel as the grave".

The grave can be cruel, and so can jealousy. Jealousy is merciless when it is directed towards those who would interfere with love. Thus God is a jealous God.

God has a burning attitude of love for His own, frequently manifesting itself as flames of fire. His love will brook no rivals. His love must be supreme in our lives. God knows if it is not, our lives will be a total loss to Him and to ourselves. So intensely does God love us that it is woe to all who would mess with that love. Not unexpectedly then the Shulamite expands upon her husband's jealous concern by using the following thought of vehement flame.

"The coals thereof are coals of fire..a most vehement

109

<u>flame."</u>

The phrase, "a most vehement flame" is often translated, "The flame of Jehovah". Talk about intensity of love! The Shulamite felt that Solomon loved her as much as God loves! That is how Christ loves the Church, and how we are to love our spouse.

How intense is your love commitment? Remember, love is no weak emotion. It is likened to the flames of God against which NOTHING can stand! It not only is strong as death, it is STRONGER than death; for it is the greatest! It will defeat anything that would frustrate God's eternal purpose for us.

Is your love commitment that strong? Does your spouse rest in the strength of your love? Remember the old hymn, "O love that will not let me go, I rest my weary soul in Thee..." Let us love as God loves, with a burning intensity.

There was a lady about ready to give up on marriage. Her husband was known as a very flirtatious person, especially at his office, and he seemed to delight in ignoring her when they were with other people. She decided that her commitment to him was not what it should be, and determined to make it as intense as possible.

The first thing she did really surprised him. When he came home from work he found a sign on the front door which said, "NO MATTER WHAT YOU DO, I WILL NEVER LEAVE YOU OR FORSAKE YOU"! He was embarrassed, and knew right away what she was getting at. He felt instant guilt about his actions, confessed it to her and told her how foolish he was and vowed his commitment to her.

LOVE IS AN INDESTRUCTIBLE COMMITMENT

<u>8:7 - "Many waters cannot quench love, neither can floods drown it".</u>

Notice she does not say that rivers and waters will not come, but that rivers and waters will not OVERCOME! Love is a waterproof torch! Should a river flow over love it will still be burning when the waters have passed. Love cannot be quenched, it cannot be destroyed. Love not only cannot be put to death, it cannot be put out.

What a wonderful description of God's love. God's love for us remains no matter what floods attempt to drown it. NOTHING can separate us from His love (Rom. 8:38-39).

How would you describe the love you possess? Is it the unquenchable kind? Evidently flood waters have quenched the love flames of many, or the flame was so weak that it sputtered out of its own accord.

Will your love commitment hold when natural beauty fades, or weight accumulates, or sickness sets in to stay, or when silver hair replaces the gold, or hard times become a miserable bedfellow? Will your love hold strong and true should your hopes and dreams become shattered? Will your love hold firm should your spouse grow indifferent? Will it hold if waywardness is found in them? Will your love hold fast if they commit adultery? Would that overwhelming flood quench your love? Will your love hold when the natural force abates in your spouse, but not in you? Is your love commitment the indestructible kind that nothing can destroy?

Let me tell you a remarkable story of love. Way back in the hill country of Ephraim there lay a small pastoral village where lived two young people. One was a young man named Hosea, the other a pretty girl named Gomer. Of course you can surmise how the story proceeds, for it has been repeated a million times. They fell madly in love and became engaged. However, for some reason, Gomer became restless and loose. Before they were to be married, Gomer was found with child. Hosea, by law, could have had her put away, or stoned for her betrayal of love. Instead he went on loving her.

Hosea took her back and married her, and three children were born. Believe it or not, Hosea did not know who the father was of either child! Finally Gomer left home for good. Apparently Hosea could not afford the luxuries she desired, or she had a whoring heart. All appeals for her return to home and family failed. Despite knowing her life of adultery, Hosea went on loving her. He sought her.

Finally the day came when he found her on the auction block. She has been used and misused and discarded by all. Now she was to be sold as the sex slave for whoever had the price. Hosea paid the price of her redemption and took her home again where he lovingly cared for her. Eventually she was physically and emotionally restored.

Probably she never understood why Hosea's flame of love for her still burned, but she could never deny that he loved her. Hosea had a persevering love, one that was indestructible. He loved like God loves. Nor can we understand why God should keep loving us, and seeking us, when we have hurt and grieved Him so. But He does, for He loves us with an everlasting love. His commitment to us never changes.

LOVE IS AN INVALUABLE COMMITMENT

8:7 - "If a man would give all the substance of his house for love, it would utterly be contemned".

Solomon has set forth for us that Love is Boundless, Deathless, Quenchless, and now he presents it as Priceless.

Love carries no price tag. Sex can be bought, but not love. Love must be given. Solomon declares that if a man gave all he had to buy love, he would be utterly contemned (DESPISED)! And rightly so.

Why should that man be despised? Because he has no understanding of what love is, and because he has underestimated its value. He would be despised because he had reduced love to a matter of barter, and the person from which it comes to an object. Even to set the price of love at a billion dollars would reduce it to nothing, for love, by its very nature, must be given.

Husbands cannot buy love by the giving of things. That may be thoughtful, but love is built on stronger stuff than "things". It flows from the heart, not the pocketbook.

If a man offered a woman all his wealth for her love it would be an insult. It would be a cruel attempt to depersonalize her. For her to accept price would be her greatest degradation, for in reality it would make her love as legalized prostitution.

Love is priceless, it cannot be purchased!

LOVE IS PRICELESS BECAUSE THE ONE WHO IS LOVED IS PRICELESS!

Chapter Twelve

FORMING FIRM FOUNDATIONS

Necessity is laid upon married couples to so live and love that they produce in their children qualities and character that will make their future wedded life a correct and complete one. Solomon and the Shulamite had been prepared in advance for the most meaningful relationship of life.

Solomon sets forth in this chapter the truth that personal character is crucial to a lasting commitment. When an individual is not controlled by integrity, commitments are not kept and promises are not fulfilled. One may go through the marriage motions, say all the proper words, but apart from strong moral character the vows are usually broken. If one is not strong in heart, they are generally weak in commitment.

Solomon provides us a flashback into the background of the Shulamite that gives an insight into her charming character. He emphasizes that the important thing is what a person is inside. The inner being is more essential to love and marriage than all the outward attractions of a beautiful body.

In these next verses we gain a glimpse as to how the character of the Shulamite was developed through a strong family background, along with a sense of personal worth.

8:8 - "We have a little sister..."

The first thing Solomon touches on is the family background. She had a family that cared enough for her to dispense discipline and proper values.

We had already met her brothers in passing (1:6); but here they are doing the speaking. Apparently the father had passed away and they have taken charge of family affairs.

"She hath no breasts"

They had looked upon her as immature; thus their strong feeling of responsibility. Doubtless this was said when she was not yet a teen.

"What shall we do for our sister in the day when she shall be spoken for?"

They began to ponder what should be done to prepare her for marriage. It is a most serious matter, and foundation building must begin early. It takes love and long preparation.

8:9 - "If she be a wall, we will build upon her a palace of silver".

A plan of preparation is devised. "If she be a wall" means that if she proves virtuous, and strong against advances of suitors, they will reward her by improving on what is already good. Like a decorative battlement of silver that would increase the beauty of a wall, they would build to increase the beauty of her character.

"And if she be a door, we will enclose her with boards of cedar."

Everything hinged on whether she would be a wall or an open door. If she were a door open to advances they would have to be strict with her in order to keep her from damaging her life for marriage. Their desire was that her life not only give forth a pleasing fragrance, but that inwardly she be incorrupted. Cedar is a wood that not only emits a lasting fragrance, but deters moths, etc., from despoiling that which is held within.

The fact that the family was concerned about this matter reveals their importance in character development, as well as in character protection.

Thus the decision was made to reward or discipline their sister as needed. Discipline and encouragement take the kind of time that only love will give. And they loved her enough to do it; enough to do their part.

8:10 - "I am a wall, and my breasts like towers".

Let us commend her in that she did her part too! She

chose to be a wall! The words, "my breasts like towers" reveal that she feels she is a grown woman and sees herself as mature. The fact that she also confesses to being "a wall" indicates her moral integrity. She had kept herself pure; therefore she had the needed respect for herself to produce a good self image.

"Then was I in his eyes as one that found favour".

This conveys the thought that she also had the respect of others. When she became a fine looking woman, it was "THEN" that Solomon became impressed with her. She had become such a person that in his eyes she found "favour" (Peace)!

She uses here a familiar expression in Scripture, though she slightly changes it, "to find grace in one's eyes". It refers to finding favor before someone, like Noah "found grace in the eyes of the Lord". In this case, however, it suggests a woman finding love in the eyes of a man! She is saying that when Solomon looked upon her she saw more than love in his eyes, she saw PEACE! She could rest in him. "THEN was I in his eyes..." Oh the first time I saw you!

"My breasts were as towers".

The emphasis is not on size, but on strength! She made her personal choice to remain undefiled for the one she would marry, and, in spite of her physical attractiveness she maintained and developed moral integrity and strength.

8:11 - "Solomon had a vineyard at Baal-hammon; he let out the vineyards unto keepers".

It seems Solomon is letting us in on where they first met. Solomon must have rented his vineyard to her brothers, and they in turn put her to work in it. Work in no way harms a teenager. In fact it greatly helps in the development of their character. Plus it keeps them occupied and out of trouble at a critical time in their lives. The brothers saw to it that she did not have much time or opportunity to meet the boys.

However, as good fortune dictated, it was more than just a "vineyard". It belonged to the King! And like any concerned property owner he kept his eye on his property and the tenants. One day when he passed by the vineyard he was impressed with the exhilarative realization that the landscape had vastly improved and was lovelier than ever. One of the grape pickers made him take a second look, then a third, etc. It was "THEN" the Shulamite became in his eyes as one who finds favor. Soon after she passed from the work of the vineyard to the wonder of the palace, and a share in the glory of Solomon's throne.

"Every one for the fruit thereof was to bring a thousand pieces of silver".

This simply refers to the rent paid Solomon for the use of his vineyards.

8:12 - "My vineyard, which is mine, is before me".

Some wonder what vineyard this is. It appears she is referring to HERSELF (1:6, 2:15). To put it in the present day vernacular she is saying, "Solomon, you possess much, but my vineyard is the best vineyard you have." While it may be his, it still is hers.

Marriage does not mean the wife ceases to be herself. It does mean, however, that while she knows she belongs to her husband, she still chooses to freely give herself. The following words say so much.

"O Solomon, must have a thousand"!

The Shulamite is willingly giving the value of her own person to her husband. It is as though she says, "Now I am your vineyard, and I give the entire worth of my possession to you, I withhold nothing. I give myself freely to you. It is my right and choice to do this!"

"And those that keep the fruit thereof two hundred".

How sweetly she suggests that he should not forget that he owes something to those who took care of her vineyard. Her family kept her vineyard for him, and he should feel indebted to them. She is simply asking Solomon to recognize the value of what he has received in her as a Bride, and to appreciate the role her family played in making it all possible.

This again reveals more of the depth of her character. The Shulamite was not the type of person to forget and forsake her family after she became successful and moved from the obscurity of poverty to the ovations of the palace, where she shared in the kingly glory of the throne of Solomon.

8:13 - "Thou that dwellest in the gardens".

Oh how utterly beautiful! Here the bridegroom is voicing his last known desire for his bride. He is rejoicing in the fact that she is now dwelling where he dwelt. She is abiding in the gardens, the place of fruitfulness, while she awaits his soon coming. She is still building on the foundation that had been laid.

"The companions hearken to thy voice; cause me to hear it".

Once before Solomon had mentioned that he loved to hear her voice (2:14). Now there are others who love to listen to her voice as she tells of the bridegroom's beauty and glory. Perhaps this is a picture of the oriental custom of the bride and her maidens awaiting the bridegroom's appearing.

Still Solomon waits to near her voice, what she has to say concerning him, and what she feels in her heart for him. He is saying, in effect, "Don't just tell others what you think of me, tell me!" He needed to hear her praise too.

Is it not remarkable that at the conclusion of this Song the husband is still longing, with the same burning intensity of early courtship, to grow in the knowledge and understanding of his fascinating wife! So it ought to be with every marriage. We sing of our Lord, "The longer I serve Him, the sweeter He grows." And every husband and wife should be able to say, "The longer I know them, the sweeter they grow."

8:14 - "Make haste, my beloved, and be thou like to a roe or to a young hart upon the mountains of spices."

Love has at last accomplished its desired work. The heart of the bride is now entirely occupied with him. With a full heart the Shulamite cries, "Make haste, my beloved." How deeply she longs for him. Only his immediate presence can satisfy.

She reveals no sign of being apathetic or indifferent toward her husband. She is not slow to respond concerning her need of him. There is a time "to make haste" in love. It must be thus if marital courtship is to survive and continue to grow. Who could possibly estimate the value of love and romance in marriage? They are the imperatives that put music to the words. They are what make us pray that the song may never end! They build for us those lasting memories. They are the spices that make a right marriage so desirable and successful.

It is a like need for our Lord Jesus that causes the loving heart to longingly cry, "Even so come quickly"! And when He comes we shall be ushered out of this earthly garden and into His presence on the mountain of SPICES! Are those spices not our Lord's infinite merits which perfume all of Heaven? The foul corruption of our sins will never be perceptible before those great mountains of fragrant spices. No wonder we long for our Lord to return quickly. We want to be taken out of these lowlands and to the high mountains of spices.

So we leave the bride in the gardens, surrounded by companions who delight to hear her speak of her beloved. This is the last picture we have of the Bride. As such it is wonderfully significant. She is seen witnessing and waiting in the gardens as she anticipates the soon coming of her absent Lord and Lover.

Chapter Thirteen

HOW DOES YOUR GARDEN GROW?

8:13 - "Thou that dwellest in the gardens..hearken to my voice"!

Falling in love for some is like falling in a deep ditch. You may have found it so. Perhaps somewhere in days distant you thought true love had come your way. Then things went awry, and what happened in that relationship turned sour and keeps you bitter and beaten, depressed and devastated. To this day you remain beset with the gnawing pain of having been deceived and discarded. And somehow you blame God that it ever happened.

Or it may be that love beckoned and you proudly married. The future looked as promising as a bright spring morning. Every flower was abloom, and every bird was singing in your garden. Then what you believed to be the eternal flame of love turned your dream castle into heaps of ashes. Nothing major may have caused the upheaval. It was probably little molehills that suddenly became gigantic mountains. Conversation became unreasonable and unbearable. Inconsideration, indifference and intolerance did their part. Neither party was giving or forgiving. You still feel bitterness surging deep within. Perhaps the gall of bitterness has so affected your heart that you are convinced you were not, or are not, the kind of person your spouse deserved or needs; that you are insensitive, impatient, incompatible or impure. Furthermore, you have tried to convince yourself that it is absolutely impossible to sing Solomon's Song.

Northwinds brought chilling blasts into your life, and divorce or death has left emotional scars and loneliness. People parade across your memory who seem to have evaded such problems and hurts. Conscience, like a goad, points to the Shulamite and Solomon, and you find yourself saying, "Their marriage got better and better, but mine is ruined. They still had each other; but for me life is over." You may even have become persuaded that you have gone beyond the reach of God's helping hand. Yet your heart cries for help and you wonder if there is such a thing as help for you. Oh there is! A greater than Solomon is here!

Suppose I were the Number One Horticulturist in the world, and someone had wrecked my garden. The green grass refuses to grow, and the once lovely flowers seem reluctant to bloom. Without argument my superior knowledge and experience as the best horticulturist qualifies me as the one to bring the garden back to normalcy. I could not undo what had been done, but I could redo. Because the garden belonged to me I could accept the problem and set about restoring it to fruitfulness and beauty.

Your garden belongs to the One greater than Solomon. He created you. He knows all about you. He understands your innermost feelings, your deepest hurts, your humiliating experiences. Because He is God, He alone possesses the knowledge and ability to minister your restoration and recovery. And because He loves you, He is ready and willing to help. Even now He is waiting for you to come to Him.

Years ago another hurting person found this true of our Lord. It happened to be a woman caught in the act of adultery. Her garden had been violated. She was actually the unwitting pawn of some religious hypocrites who wanted to use her to trap the Lord in His own words. She became the scapegoat in their test case. Surely it was their design for they let the far worse offender, the man, go free.

With wicked hands they dragged her before the Lord. Thrown at His feet, she lay embarrassed and dishonored. Her head was lowered with guilt and shame, as a flower with broken petals. Tears like unchecked rivers flowed down her cheeks.

The uncaring accusers said, "The Law says stone her! What do you say?" Doesn't that sound like some church members? They knew they had the support of the Law behind them, and that the Lord would have to correctly answer, "Stone her". With smug silence they waited to hear how this compassionate Christ would reply.

Do you know what our lovely Lord did? He stooped down and calmly wrote in the sand. He did not look at the woman; perhaps because the pureness of His eyes would only have pierced her heart with deeper shame. His compassion however was absolutely genuine. Then He said, "He that is without sin among you, let him cast the first stone". To their great consternation He had not disagreed with the Law! And while he was speaking He was writing in the sand. I believe He wrote different sins those men had committed. And beginning with the eldest (because he could recognize more of the sins), they all left. When only He and the woman remained, Jesus said, "Where are thine accusers?" She told Him there were none, and then He said, "Neither do I condemn thee, go and sin no more."

Slowly her head lifted, and she looked into the gentle eyes of One she knew spoke with love, grace and truth. She realized forgiveness, and her face radiated with hope. She had not been condemned for what had transpired in her life. SHE HAD BEEN FORGIVEN! Perhaps her head bowed again, but this time in worship.

Our Lord did not violate or void His Law. He overcame it with a higher law, the Law of Forgiveness. He accepted the woman just as she was, broken and bitter, and forgave her. Her future obedience would determine the extent of healing for the past. It would also determine how enriched her new life would become in the future.

Where does restoration and recovery begin when life is full of hurts? The words may sound familiar, but how can one put music to them? Is there help when the well is dry and the garden knows no dew? There is nothing anyone can do. That is, there is nothing anyone can do alone. Help is needed! The help of God is needed! And that is where hope springs highest. There is the Groundsman, the Divine Husbandman, who is the Keeper of the gardens. He knows how to help and restore. He is the Healer of broken hearts, the Mender of marriages, the Lifter of fallen lives. And that One cares for you!

If the Almighty God could take a world so run amuck in chaos, so formless there remained no semblance of structure, and restore it to its original beauty and order, then surely He can take your damaged and defeated life and make something beautiful out of it. The slumbering chords can vibrate once more, and sweeter music than ever will issue forth. You can sing the song again!

There is no doubt about that for the Lord Himself told us. He even explained it. He taught that our little well could become a river of living waters, forever springing up within us. It was a picture of Him living and working in the believer.

Remember that hot day in Samaria when our Lord was resting on Jacob's well? That was when He provided another wonderful illustration of this truth. Through the heat of the noon day sun a woman slowly approached the well. She came at noon, while others were resting, that she might avoid embarrassment. She was an outcast of society, and thus there was hesitancy upon finding someone at the well. She had married five times in her pursuit of love and happiness. Each time she found only more disillusionment and disappointment. Now she was living with the sixth man. She had drunk of the Fountain of Love, but found it forbidden and unsatisfying.

It was like drinking salt water, for she was left with a bitter taste and unquenched thirst. However, on this red letter day in her life, she would drink of Living Water. She would discover true and satisfying love. She came with a bucket in her hand, but went away with the Well in her heart.

Though that story occurred centuries ago it was repeated just recently. It happened following a mid-week service. As I walked out of church a man and woman were waiting on the steps. They were unmarried. The man said, "Preacher, she needs to talk to you!" For all the world he reminded me of those men who gladly brought the adulteress to Jesus. Upon inviting them into the study, I immediately discovered the man wanted to do all the talking. He could not wait to fill me in on her sordid life; how she had already been married five times, and even now was seeking after men. Of course she tearfully denied the accusations.

Realizing the man would only hinder any efforts to help the woman, I suggested he step out of the study so we could talk further. She sat with head bowed, face flushed with embarrassment. I felt at a loss to know what to say or do. Prompted by the Holy Spirit I opened the Word of God to the fourth chapter of the Gospel of John and read aloud the account of another lady who had had five husbands, and was living with a sixth.

While reading the story I could see tears glisten their way down her cheeks. At the part where Jesus told the lady, "Whosoever drinketh of this water shall never thirst", and of the Samaritan's request, "Give me this water that I thirst not", she looked up with hopeful astonishment, and said, "Can I drink of that water?"

How wonderful to see her drink of Living Water. She dipped in her cup and came up with the Well. That holds true of all who drink of Living Water. They drink of Christ and are satisfied. This lady went on her way rejoicing, just like the Samaritan went away rejoicing. She had met the Purifier of muddied wells, the Restorer of ravaged gardens, the Healer of broken hearts and homes.

Love never faileth! The love of man may falter and fail, but never the love of God. Nothing that has taken place, or anything that is to come, can change the love of God for His own; nor can anything separate us from His love. God's love abideth regardless of what transpires in our lives. There is no need to hide from God among your ruins. In fact God so intensely loves that He devises ways and means to bring His banished back; and sometimes we are brought back through severe storms, and over rough roads. But God's love is relentless to bring the wandering or hurting child home to forgiveness and restoration.

From our thoughts here we are not implying that only women are offenders, and in need of God's help. Being one of the male species makes it painfully aware that the balance of guilt swings heavily on our side. Nor are we remotely inferring that it is only adultery that devastates lives. Adultery does leave unforgettable hurts in hearts and homes; as perhaps nothing else does. But many things work to rob us of our dreams and delights, and drive us to depression and defeat, or leave us scarred and songless. Almost any jolt can render the instrument out of tune.

Yet, when life gets out of tune and only a medley of disharmony is forthcoming, God still ministers infinite patience and grace. It is because He has committed His love to us forever; and that love is unending, unchanging, unquenchable, and undying. You can count on it!

Because God made you, and loves you, and bought you, He will never forget or forsake you. You are His garden and His constant concern is that it bloom forever. With His help it will! Listen to the wisdom of this One called Counsellor. In obeying His words you will put music to them. And in obeying His Word your heart will once again hear the Sound of Music! You will know the joy of walking in the presence of your true Lover while living in the Land of Beginning Again!

Chapter Fourteen

TRIBUTE TO A FLOWER

(The following is a sermon delivered by the author honoring his wife on Mother's Day, just prior to their fortieth wedding anniversary. It is a timely tribute of praise. While the message is for all, there is the awareness that it is directed especially to her. It is a fitting conclusion to the study of the Song of Solomon).

Song of Solomon 2:1-2. - "I am the rose of Sharon, the lily of the valleys. As the lily among thorns, so is my love among the daughters."

This heart of mine has always felt great fascination for names found in Scripture. The names of Bible characters always prove intriguing. And what an inexhaustible study is provided us in the over four hundred designations given our lovely Lord. Thus when we find the sweet Shulamite spoken of as the Rose of Sharon, and the Lily of the Valleys, we understand those titles present her as the object of universal admiration and delight.

Among flowers the grand purple ribbon must be awarded the rose. If asked to judge and declare the Queen of Flowers we would have to place the golden crown on the royal rose. It is the ornament of earth, the splendor of plants, the beauty of the fields, and its lingering fragrance fills the air and heart with awe. Solomon saw his bride as THE rose of Sharon, and THE lily of the valleys. There was none like unto her. She was like her Lord, the Plant of Renown. Being altogether lovely, there was combined in her the qualities of them all.

That is why I have always referred to my Nellie as "The Little Flower". She has been a miniature of the Greatest Flower. She has combined the exquisite beauties of Christ in her life, and His excellent perfumes have always been manifest through her.

Adam had Eve, the Pride of Paradise. Isaac had Rebecca, the Marvel of Mesopotamia, Boaz had Ruth, the Gleaner of Grace. Solomon had the Shulamite, the Elegant of Engedi. And Keith Knauss had Nellie, the Virtuous from the Vineyards of Hunts Hollow!

Herewith I give you her tribute. It all began when a young man, flush with his first driver's license, asked his freckled-faced, pig-tailed sister to stop grape picking and ride with him to check out what was taking place in a big tent in Naples, New York. They surmised a carnival had come to town. To their surprise it turned out to be a revival meeting with a black evangelist. But through that strange circumstance both were saved, and in due time both made their way to Bible School.

That was where I blended into the picture. How incredible that I should fail to notice her those first months at school. Then, in that junior year it happened! Having been placed in charge of the Potato Crew, I was busy peeling the stay of mankind when before my window appeared a vision! My blood pressure went wild. It rose to such astronomical heights that Ripley would not have believed it, and Guinness would have questioned it. But there she stood in all her loveliness! Mother had always said I would know the right one when I saw her. I did! And God bears witness that I was not disobedient to the Heavenly Vision! My ravished heart still races when I see her. She stands out as Queen of the Crowd!

The monumental problem I faced was how to convince her she was the one for me! In God's good grace and time it was accomplished, and upon graduation we were married under an arbor of lilacs in the long-gone Church of the Open Bible near Geneva; come forty years this June First. When all the congratulations were given we drove off with tin cans tied to the bumper of a '35 Ford coupe, and our pockets filled with dreams of a life and ministry to be. Soon after, the First Baptist Church of Killawog, New York extended us a call to become their pastor. Those next five years are enhanced in our book of memories. We always wondered why the parsonage was not shown us when candidating. We found out when we moved in! And we always wondered why a couple of green kids like us were chosen over twelve experienced candidates. The reason we discovered was that the others did not want the place! The parsonage had not been blessed with paint for most of three decades, and rain water from off the hills flowed directly through the basement, and the structure sagged in places where it should not sag. That is why we had to place wedges under our plates to keep the gravy on! And nighttimes in the parsonage found a multitude of rats convening from the local feed mill to conduct wall races and sundry sacrilegious practices. Yet how excited we were that any church anywhere would call us to be their Pastor and wife. We moved to that huge home with all our earthly possessions tucked into the "rumble seat" of that old Ford coupe. We were now Pastor and Mrs. Knauss!

Dare we mention the weekly salary of twenty dollars? What more did a young couple need? After tithe was taken out that left us with eighteen dollars! Much of that went to buy gas, as the three-seater yellow taxi we purchased was also used as the church bus. How exuberant the youth were that day when twenty-eight of them rode in it. And how horrified the elders were! But you took those three dollars budgeted for groceries and somehow made them stretch even though we kept every speaker, missionary, and traveling evangelist that came along; and the revival meetings always lasted two weeks! You had a special knack of making beans and macaroni seem fit for a king.

Those years and memories are priceless. What laughs and tears we shared. Probably the most memorable time was when the heating stove ran out of fuel in the dead of winter, and we had been gone overnight. The water pipes in the upstairs lavatory had broken and the water had gathered and frozen above the living room ceiling. We arrived home in time to get the house warm before the mid-week prayer group came. How were we to know there was ice overhead, and that it was thawing out? And when the plaster gave way and the water descended into the midst of all of us, who could have imagined those deacons would react the way they did when soaking wet? It bordered on ungodliness!

Then you gave birth to our first two daughters. Now I never faulted you for going right ahead and having children even though we could not afford them, because you sure came up with two extra specials! We named the first daughter Penny so that we would never be broke again. And how good it was that God provided a doctor born and raised in the home of a country preacher. He refused to take any money for his services because he understood our situation.

That little church along the Tioughnioga tributary grew from twenty to one hundred and twenty. It even made honorable mention in the National Sunday School contest! And did not the community sit up and take notice when those huge beams were soaped and the church was slid to one side for a basement to be dug and built. How mad the Methodists were for our going one up on them!

Then came the shocking news when the doctor informed us that we would have to move to survive, or else I would lose you. You were so physically run down, and the salary did not allow us to buy the proper foods. Having two babies, and poor nutrition, had taken its toll. Plus you always took the little ones to every service and youth meeting or outing, conducted Vacation Bible School, kept every speaker who came along, and managed to maintain a semblance of sanity while living with me.

Still when the doctor told us we had to move we did not want to, for we loved those dear people. But we went to God in prayer about it and asked that if it were His will for us to move He would send an invitation for a week of meetings from a church and pastor we did not know. How we laughed at the thought of that, for nobody cared to listen to me preach who knew me, let alone someone who never heard of me. BUT GOD DID IT! God not only did it, He went beyond what we could imagine or think and sent in two such invitations! How could we doubt after that?

In the course of God's time He led us to Iowa. When we arrived to candidate, and saw the dumpy old building that small congregation was meeting in, we were convinced God had made His first blunder. But when that Sunday was over we knew those people were our people. In fact I was so sure God had led us there that we stayed over an extra day and bought needed furniture on the installment plan. I also went to the County Court House and purchased an Iowa license for our car. Then that night the incredible happened, for at their business meeting the church decided not to call us!

Remember the long ride home? You cried and I sang. You kept asking how I could sing when we had just been rejected, gone deep into debt, and our car now carried the license of a state we did not live in! I could only answer that it was because we would soon be moving to Iowa. What a day that was when the phone rang and those Iowa folks informed us they had held another meeting and voted to call us. Did you ever realize we are just a couple of RECALLS?

With our little ones in arm we moved our few belongings to Iowa and arrived flat broke to begin a ministry. And what a ministry God gave us! Soon that oddity of a church building was sold and a relocation and building program underway. Those next years witnessed four building programs, over thirty youth going into God's service, and over five hundred additions to the church! And so the story goes.

Then came that lovely day when daughter number three arrived. We now had Penny, Doris and Kim. Say, haven't we got some family! And what an example of Christian womanhood and motherhood you were before those three girls.

God allowed us the privilege to minister fourteen wonderful years to those good folks. That sure is a long time for people to put up with us. Even there you were constantly head over heels in work, supervising youth groups, directing choir, organizing and maintaining nurseries, keeping the lid on problems, involved in committees and societies, counseling, etc. Then there was that move to the Chicago area and a prestigious church where you once again were thrust into the role of Hostess, and in one year alone logged two hundred and fifty- three guests. But we saw that church relocate and build a huge new edifice and fifty members added on the first Sunday.

Remember also that wonderful ministry God gave us in Michigan. We know now why God sent us there, for our family added a super son-in-law. But it was there things caught up with us and we began to experience the consequences of burnout. When we left those gracious people they made it possible for us to enjoy a Caribbean cruise and needed rest.

God has been so good to us. Though we have known our share of hard times and hard knocks, He has made up the difference in double portions of benefits. Do you realize God has made it possible for us to visit twenty-three countries and Alaska twice! Goodness and Mercy have followed us all our days. Then too, along the way we picked up two extra ordinary grandchildren! Isn't that family of ours something special!

Still the prospects are not much better than when we began. We have little more than when we started. Retirement seems out of the question with only Social Security as sole support. But grace has brought us safe thus far and grace will lead us on. You will have to admit I never promised you a Rose Garden. You have made it along side of me for these forty years and still things do not cast a brighter glow. But I guarantee if you stick with me you will someday walk on streets of gold!

I know you have not yet got a home to call your own. For a lifetime we have returned to the churches, in rent-free parsonages, money that could have been used to purchase a home. But, after all, we are just pilgrims and the better day is coming.

Please excuse me for having digressed into memories. It is you I pay tribute to. How proud I have always been to introduce you as my wife. You always prove so gracious and considerate, wise and mannerly, and always look so lovely.

You stood by me when anyone lesser would have given up, left and never looked back. You stuck with me when the cupboards were bare, the pockets empty, and the storms raging.

Looking back over those years of ministry together I cannot point out a single instance when you were anything less than you should have been before the churches. I found no fault in you, nor did anyone else. I have never heard anyone say ought against you. Everyone who knows you thinks and speaks the highest of you. Everywhere and in every way you complimented my ministry. You made our life and home border on Heaven. Oh, the magic of your touch, the marvel of your words, the ministry of your love, and the music of your home.

Let me confess that I would never have made it without you. And if I had to do it all over again, I would plead with God to give me you. You always have been an example of the Believer, and the model of a pastor's wife. Somehow you always knew what to say, how to say it, and when. Your speech is always seasoned with grace.

Much of your labor of love has been unseen, unheralded, and unrewarded. How often you have gone into homes of the needy and given groceries to help hard-put families. And no one will ever know the countless hours you spend in counseling troubled ladies who have found in you a true confidant.

You have labored alongside of me without regard to compensation. And most people expected far more from you than from me. The cares of the church have come daily upon you as well. Yet you have stayed the same sweet person. There must have been times when you found it difficult to remain sweet and gracious, for too often the pious "daughters of Jerusalem" communicate to you their carnal discontent over your husband's visitation and administration and while they are at it, make sure you understand who is the latest in the flock to have their feelings hurt; all of course under the guise of it being something they feel you should know. Still you treat them all with grace, for that is the kind of person you are.

However, through the years, there have been many who reckoned you a blessing and benefit to the church, and not a sounding board. They were thankful for such a pastor's wife. They needed you, befriended you, made you feel part of their lives, took you places, desired your friendship and fellowship. But whether they did or not, you treated them all with the graciousness so befitting you.

Pretty little lady, you are such an unusual person and such a precious gift. Is it any wonder that I love you? How great is your love and suffering comingled?

Without doubt the ministry is the most lonely of places; especially for the pastor's wife. She must remain the solid rock of comfort and counsel for others, while her own griefs and hurts go unattended. No one walks that lonely road with greater heaviness of heart; often feeling like the Lord, an outsider among her own people. Many receive her not! Folks fail to remember, or recognize, that she is as called of God to the ministry as her husband.

How often I have found you crying in the privacy of some room, and you would not tell me why. But I knew some razor sharp tongue had done its devastating work, and I also knew you had not returned evil for evil, but rendered kindness instead, for that is the sort of person you are.

Solomon said, "Other daughters have done well, but thou excellest them all!" Lovely lady, that must be said of you! You have supplied the harmony in this preacher's home, and furnished the fragrance in his garden. You have graced this life of mine, the lives of our family, and the lives of all you touch. You are that one-in-a-million person. You are the Total Woman!

Mrs. Noah was also a preacher's wife. She faithfully went about her work and raised her family true to God. They were the only boys worth saving when the flood came. She kept a home that was not always a home; it was like a traveling zoo for quite awhile She stood by her preacher-man through one hundred twenty years of fruitless and unappreciated ministry. She stood true to God even when her husband failed and fell.

There was a time in this old cursed world when the greatest person alive was the wife of a preacher; and I know for a fact that it is still that way today. You belong to that select group of whom God declares, "the world is not worthy!"

Fairest Flower of them all, how I love you! I find no spot in you. You are altogether lovely! You have done me nothing but good. Your price is beyond earth's rarest rubies! You have crowned my life with diadems of deity. I live like a King!

Is there no sense of protocol? Please rise. Render unto this Rose of Sharon, this Lily among thorns, the honor due her. Acclaim her rightful royalty. Ye men remove your hats! Ye ladies bend the knee! Ye youth stand in awed reverence! Ye children clap your hands! The Queen of Queens is being escorted by on the arm of her husband!

BIBLIOGRAPHY

Aardsma, J. Allen and Walter J. Black, But Comely. Veritas
    Biblical Research Center: West Sayville, New York, 1977.

Burrowes, George. The Song of Solomon. The Banner Of Truth
    Trust: London, reprinted 1958.

Clarke, Arthur G. The Song of Songs. Walterick Publishers:
    Kansas City, 1957.

Dillow, Joseph G. Solomon On Sex. Thomas Nelson: Nashville
    1977.

Fowler, Clifton L. Song Of Solomon. Maranatha Press: Lincoln.
    1967.

Ginsburg, Christain D. The Song Of Songs. Reed and Pardon:
    London, 1857.

Halff, Charles. The Song Of Solomon. The Christian Jew Hour:
    San Antonio, 1964.

Ironside, H. A. Addresses On The Song Of Solomon. Loizeaux
    Brothers: New York, 1943.

Lockyer, Herbert. Love Is Better Than Wine. New Leaf Press:
    Harrison, AK., 1981.

Loveless, Wendell P. Christ And The Believer In The Song Of
    Songs. Moody Press: Chicago, 1945.

McPhee, L.M. The Romance Of The Ages. Designed Products:
    Oak Ridge, Il., 1950.

Mason, Clarence E. Love Song. Moody Press: Chicago, 1976.

Nee, Watchman. Song Of Songs. Christian Literature Crusade: Fort Washington, P.A., 1965.

Neighbour, R. E. The Song Of Songs Which Is Solomon's. Union Gospel Press: Cleveland, 1927.

Penn-Lewis, Jessie. Thy Hidden Ones. Overcomer Literature Trust: Dorset, England, 1957.

Rust, E. A. An Exposition Of The Song Of Solomon. Rust: 1939.

Shelton, L. R. My Beloved. Old Puritan Press: New Orleans, 1958.

Taylor, J. Hudson, Union And Communion. Dimension Books: Minneapolis.

Ward, A. G. Song Of Solomon. Gospel Publishing House: Springfield, 1935.

Webber, Charles and David. The Song Of Solomon. Zondervan Publishing House: Grand Rapids, 1962.